THE
POWER OF
BASKETBALL

THE
POWER OF
BASKETBALL

NBA Players, Coaches, and Team Governors on the Fight to Make a Better America

EDITED BY
NATIONAL BASKETBALL SOCIAL JUSTICE
COALITION, JAMES CADOGAN & ED CHUNG

THE
NEW
PRESS

NEW YORK
LONDON

Requests for permission to reproduce selections from this book should be
made through our website: https://thenewpress.com/contact.

Published in the United States by The New Press, New York, 2024

Distributed by Two Rivers Distribution

ISBN 978-1-62097-921-1 (hc)
ISBN 978-1-62097-922-8 (ebook)

CIP data is available

The New Press publishes books that promote and enrich public
discussion and understanding of the issues vital to our
democracy and to a more equitable world. These books are
made possible by the enthusiasm of our readers; the support
of a committed group of donors, large and small; the
collaboration of our many partners in the independent media and the
not-for-profit sector; booksellers, who often hand-sell New Press books;
librarians; and above all by our authors.

www.thenewpress.com

Composition by Dix Digital Prepress and Design

Printed in the United States of America

2 4 6 8 10 9 7 5 3 1

Not everything that is faced can be changed, but nothing can
be changed until it is faced.
—*James Baldwin*

No group has had more influence on society—and on
me—than athletes.
—*Kareem Abdul-Jabbar*

If you can take something to levels that very few other people
can reach, then what you're doing becomes art.
—*Bill Russell*

———————————————————————

*The National Basketball Social Justice Coalition and the
work it supports would not exist without George Hill, Lebron
James, Chris Paul, and the brotherhood of NBA players
across the league. Their leadership in 2020 anchored the
NBA community—and the world of sports—at a time when
only courage could hope to meet the moment and pave the
way for a brighter future.*

CONTENTS

Foreword by Adam Silver & Andre Iguodala   ix

Introduction by James Cadogan & Ed Chung   1

1. Steve Ballmer, *No Time to Waste*   9

2. J. B. Bickerstaff, *Doing the Work*   21

3. Malcolm M. Brogdon, *The Question That Drives Me*   33

4. Caron Butler, *Telling My Story for Good*   49

5. Tre Jones, *For Our Children*   63

6. CJ McCollum, *Finding the Path*   77

7. Jamahl Mosley, *Strong Communities in Action*   89

8. Larry Nance Jr., *Fighting Hunger, One Day at a Time*   97

9. Vivek Ranadivé, *Keeping Our Promises*   111

10. Glenn "Doc" Rivers, *Learning from History*   119

11. Tierra Ruffin-Pratt, *The Time Is Now*   133

12. Clara Wu Tsai, *The Business of Doing Justice*   147

Acknowledgments   159

Notes   161

FOREWORD

Sports are often used as a lens to address broader issues in society. For the NBA, standing up for fundamental principles of equality and justice have been part of the league's DNA since its earliest days.

The history of activism in the NBA dates back to trailblazers like Bill Russell, Oscar Robertson, and Kareem Abdul-Jabbar, who fiercely advocated for racial equality and social justice. They used the recognition they achieved through basketball to draw attention to important matters that impacted not only players in the league but our country. That tradition of speaking out has been passed down to future generations of NBA players whose voices and platforms have only grown in size and stature.

In 2020, NBA players—together with other members of the NBA and WNBA communities—joined the nationwide movement for racial justice following the murder of George Floyd. At that difficult and uncertain time, with the backdrop of a deadly global pandemic and operating from the NBA "bubble" in Orlando, Florida, the NBA and National Basketball Players Association came together to create two new organizations to promote social justice and economic opportunity: the National Basketball Social Justice Coalition and the NBA Foundation. These joint efforts between NBA teams and players are leading our ongoing work to create meaningful and sustainable change around issues of race and inequality.

The collection of essays on the following pages speaks to how members of the NBA family have continued the teams' and players' long-standing tradition of pursuing social justice and equality through basketball. They are using the game and its influence to bridge divides in our communities and create a forum for critical discussion and debate about a path forward—with the ultimate goal of bringing disparate people closer together.

That is the power of basketball.

Adam Silver
Commissioner
National Basketball
Association

Andre Iguodala
Executive Director
National Basketball Players
Association

INTRODUCTION

JAMES CADOGAN & ED CHUNG

Hoop Dreams to Hope

Basketball is an obsession for both of us.

As children of the 1980s and 1990s, it's the sport we grew up on. The one we played on driveways, on playgrounds, and in school gyms. Like millions of other kids across the country and around the world, we harbored dreams of one day playing ball in the NBA; sinking the game-winning buzzer-beater in Game 7 of the Finals in front of a sold-out crowd.

Instead, it was reality that sank in soon enough and we both knew we'd never lace up sneakers for a living. But our fandom never died. NBA players were still larger than life to us—literally. We both had posters of our idols on our bedrooms walls and followed them religiously: watching games and highlights on TV and checking box scores in newspapers; and then, as digital infrastructure grew, consuming everything we could online. We've seen the explosive growth of the game we love across the globe—and we've grown alongside it.

While professional basketball was beyond our reach, another passion was certainly within it—the pursuit of social and racial justice. To us, experiencing the privileges of growing up, going to school, building careers, and raising families in the United States only highlights how both of our stories are rarer than they should be, and that a long road remains to overcome some of the most intractable and systemic injustices facing too many people in our country today—especially those that disproportionately impact Black and brown communities.

Our personal stories converged when we had the opportunity to work alongside each other at the U.S. Department of Justice during the administration of President Barack Obama. It was at that time the movement to end mass incarceration and transform our criminal justice systems exploded onto the national stage. Now, in our respective leadership positions at the National Basketball Social Justice Coalition and the Vera Institute of Justice, we continue to press for meaningful policy changes that will advance social and racial justice; create safer and healthier communities with holistic interventions; ensure our criminal justice systems are accountable to the people they are supposed to serve; and promote civic participation in our democracy.

For us, that's a real dream.

Inspiring Action

Building on the long-standing institutional partnership between Vera and the NBA, we are excited to team up once again in serving as the editors for this project.

In this essay collection, a diverse array of leaders across the NBA community dive deeply into the origins of their commitment to the social justice work that have become hallmarks of their public lives. Whether as athlete, coach, or team governor, each of the authors is using their position and resources to be a leader in their community as well as in the sports, media, and entertainment industries.

It's common for high-profile figures to be reduced and flattened in the public eye: identified with a few images, soundbites, or commentary from others. That's true of leaders across the NBA family—especially players. But they are all full human beings just like the rest of us. They are parents, children, siblings, friends, and neighbors whose life experiences and worldviews are as varied, subtle, complex, and dynamic as everybody else's. But, through the unprecedented reach of today's social and digital platforms, many of those individuals now share parts of their personal lives directly with the world.

In 2020, the world saw just how powerful the humanity of the NBA community on full display could be.

When George Floyd in Minneapolis and Breonna Taylor in Louisville were killed by police that year and millions flooded into the streets to demand real accountability for police misconduct and concrete action to transform the criminal justice system, the NBA family stood alongside them. The 2020 season was ongoing in the NBA and WNBA's COVID-19 quarantine facilities colloquially known as "the Bubble" and "the Wubble." The NBA and WNBA, along with the National Basketball Players Association (NBPA) and Women's National Basketball Players Association (WNBPA), worked together to show solidarity with the movement sweeping the nation that "Black Lives Matter": The leagues unabashedly affirmed that message as players wore jerseys with impact phrases replacing their names during games broadcast around the world and player and coach media availabilities focused on social justice issues rather than just on basketball. In July, the WNBA announced it was dedicating its 2020 season to social justice and created the WNBA Social Justice Council as well as the Justice Movement platform.

Weeks later, after Jacob Blake was shot in Kenosha, Wisconsin, during the Playoffs in the Bubble, players joined the renewed national outcry and the Milwaukee Bucks did not take the floor for their scheduled game. The NBA ultimately suspended all games while players, coaches, and team governors worked through the best ways to respond to the moment. Building on the recent creation of the NBA Foundation, through which the NBA's Board of Governors committed $300 million to support greater economic opportunity in the Black community, the NBA made three new commitments with the players' support: (1) converting NBA arenas and facilities available into safe registration and polling locations in the 2020 elections given COVID-19 restrictions; (2) unprecedented league-wide action to promote civic engagement and expand voter access; and (3) the creation of a new entity, the National Basketball Social Justice Coalition.

Turning People Power into Public Policy

The creation of the Social Justice Coalition was an unprecedented joint venture by a men's major sports league and its union. Beyond the power of the NBA community's existing impact philanthropy and community-based programming, the Coalition was established to actively support policies and legislation that advance social and racial justice at the local, state, and federal levels.

At its core, the theory of the case is that, through the Coalition, the NBA community could take the historic and revolutionary moment of people power we saw in 2020 and help turn it into the public policy that impacted communities so desperately need. Led by a governing board composed of five NBA players, five team governors, two head coaches, the NBA commissioner and deputy commissioner, and the NBPA executive director, the organization has four core priorities:

- Combat mass incarceration, shrink America's prison system, and support reentry
- Promote public health approach to violence prevention and intervention
- Protect the first right of democracy by strengthening access to the ballot for all
- Advance equitable, consistent, safe, and transparent policing practices

The urgent need to address each of these areas persists today. Our criminal justice systems continue to overincarcerate with nearly two million people—disproportionately Black Americans—currently in jails and prisons. This is an increase of 500 percent over the last fifty years, and research shows that long sentences of incarceration have not had any lasting impact in reducing crime.[1] The harms of the justice system are exacerbated especially if the actors who are tasked with upholding it are not held to account. Since 2010, more than $1.5 billion has been spent to settle claims of police misconduct.[2] Our communities deserve to be safe from the gun violence that claims over 40,000 lives each year. And access to the mechanisms of our democracy—especially the ability to vote for the leaders who make these important public policy decisions—should be expanded and not suppressed. Unfortunately, in 2023 alone, lawmakers passed at least seventeen bills in fourteen states to restrict access to voting.

The Coalition stood up operations in 2021, and, at the time of this writing, had just celebrated three years of active work across the NBA community: in that time, it has driven an affirmative advocacy agenda supporting twenty-eight different pieces of legislation at the federal, state, and local levels, and helping eight of them win passage. Over that same period, leveraging the NBA's global media platform and cultural heft, the Coalition has hosted or cohosted twenty-three issue-based impact events in NBA markets across the country and brought visibility to justice issues through thousands of print media hits and reaching more than 20 million people through social channels. As part of its model, the Coalition has also worked to support dozens of leaders across the NBA community and built partnerships with more than seventy-five national and local advocacy organizations.

The Power of Basketball

Like any good team, the strength of the Social Justice Coalition is its members. And this book is designed to provide insight into why the athletes, coaches, and team governors featured here have such a personal commitment to social and racial justice. Some are Coalition board members, others are not. All are blazing a trail that others can follow.

A former all-star player and now an assistant coach with the Miami Heat, Caron Butler looks back on his incredible journey from the streets to stardom. New Orleans Pelicans forward Larry Nance Jr. shares his deep work to address food insecurity in Louisiana. Clara Wu Tsai, Governor of the New York Liberty, talks about how her life experiences show up as a philanthropist committed to Brooklyn's well-being. Milwaukee Bucks Head Coach Doc Rivers reflects on the challenges he has faced and overcome as a legendary player and coach. LA Clippers Chairman Steve Ballmer discusses the urgent need to end gun violence that is devastating whole communities. CJ McCollum, president of the NBPA and guard for the Pelicans, dissects juvenile justice and the paths we choose. J. B. Bickerstaff meditates on his father's life and influence. Tre Jones of the San Antonio Spurs tackles the lasting trauma of gun violence and the potential of violence intervention programs. Sacramento Kings Chairman Vivek Ranadivé reflects on how sports teams can support communities in their times of need. Orlando Magic Head Coach Jamahl Mosley lifts up access to the ballot and the importance of strong communities. Retired WNBA star Tierra Ruffin-Pratt talks about the impact police violence had on her life during her journey to becoming a professional athlete. And Portland Trail Blazers guard Malcolm Brogdon pens an essay tracing his family's singular legacy of social activism.

Instead of focusing solely on the ins and outs of specific policies and their research basis, this book deliberately takes the human approach. Each chapter centers the individual first—sharing, in the author's own words, the background and experiences that motivate them to commit so deeply the work of systemic change. Some of these stories have been told before, but never quite like this.

There is history here.

Members of the NBA family have always been some of the brightest lights on the front lines of the fight for equality in this country. The late Bill Russell was a civil rights champion working for justice and marching alongside Dr. Martin Luther King Jr.

during the civil rights movement of the 1960s. Oscar Robertson fought for economic justice and forever changed the business of sports. Kareem Abdul-Jabbar dedicated his life and continues to fight for racial and religious equality. They are just three of the most well-known among many others, past and present. The National Basketball Social Justice Coalition stands on the shoulders of these giants.

Our hope is that, after reading these essays, you will see each of these authors for more than their ability to drain logo threes, call the perfect inbounds play in crunch time, or build a winning franchise. Rather, we hope you'll be energized by each of these leaders' personal stories. And that their sincere commitment to positively impacting the world will motivate you do the same.

After all, what great social change has ever happened without great inspiration?

1

NO TIME TO WASTE

STEVE BALLMER

Chairman, Los Angeles Clippers
Co-Founder, Ballmer Group
Board, National Basketball Social Justice Coalition

How I Got Here

It's no secret that I'm a numbers guy.

After I retired from Microsoft in 2014, I shifted my focus to sports and philanthropy. I became chairman of the Los Angeles Clippers and set out to do everything in my power to ensure that the team would win. I also joined my wife, Connie, in philanthropy, cofounding what is now called Ballmer Group, which supports efforts to improve economic mobility and create opportunity in the U.S.

I'll admit that at first, I was skeptical about the role of philanthropy. I had assumed that the federal government already ensured that disadvantaged people—especially kids—were adequately cared for. My wife did not outright laugh in my face, but she did push me to look more closely at the hurdles, gaps, and realities faced by many families in our country—and to think about how philanthropy could help.

I wanted to understand for myself—and so I started looking at the numbers. I wanted to know where government money was going, what the outcomes of its investments were, and where Connie and I could use our resources to make a difference. The end result of my curiosity was USAFacts,[1] which examines the government's data and makes it free, widely available, and understandable.

But those weren't the only numbers I looked at. I also dug into numbers that taught me that economic mobility—a person's probability to move up the economic ladder from where they were at birth—is low. Black men and boys face the starkest challenges.[2] The government was doing plenty—but even so, too many young people were being left behind. When I learned all of this, I knew I wanted to step up and contribute.

Economic Mobility

At Ballmer Group, we believe that all young people should have the opportunity to succeed—regardless of their race, circumstances, or where they grow up. Much of our grantmaking focuses on what we call cradle to career points, the periods in a life where opportunity is created or denied—like early childhood, the school years, and young adulthood. We work in areas including education, college and career, housing, mental health, child welfare, criminal justice reform—and public safety. We believe in the power of data and technology, of advocacy, and of communities coming together to create change. From the beginning, our investments have been informed by conversations with community leaders about what is holding people and communities back. It was clear that without addressing the impact of racism, it would be impossible to improve economic mobility.

As part of this exploration, we heard a lot about the crisis of gun violence affecting Black and brown urban communities— everyday violence that usually doesn't get covered in the news. I often think about the time our executive director for Los Angeles & National Public Safety took Connie and me around LA to get a better sense of the impact our investments could make. One of the stops was Markham Middle School, where she pointed out a "berm"—or raised strip of land running the length of its soccer field. Much to our surprise, she explained that, rather than just being a piece of landscaping, the berm functioned as a shield for children to drop behind in order to protect themselves from gunfire.[3] This trip underscored the safety challenges that kids face— challenges that are as foundational as school or job prospects. If it's not safe for students to get to school, even the best academic resources and programs will not reach them.

We also met with a leading gang interventionist in LA, who talked about his work with the Watts Gang Task Force: a group of community residents including former gang members, as well as nonprofits and members of law enforcement, who meet on a regular basis to work on strategies to keep the community safe. Conversations like this shaped our understanding that effective safety efforts are often led by community members and not just the police.

These stories and conversations stuck with us. So did the data: From 2019 to 2020, deaths caused by gun violence rose 30 percent. The following year, they rose another 7 percent, to almost 21,000 deaths. Forty-two percent of that total was young Black men under the age of thirty-five.[4] When I heard this, I was stunned. As a Team Governor in the NBA, a league where 70 percent of players are Black men, I felt extra motivated by the situation.

Gun Violence in Communities

Gun violence disproportionately affects Black people in the U.S., and there are too many awful statistics to choose from that prove it. Data shows that while Black Americans made up just 12.5 percent of the U.S. population in 2020, they were the victims in 61 percent of all gun homicides that year.[5] And according to another recent study based on publicly available data, young Black males 18–24 "are nearly 23 times more likely to die by firearm homicide than their white male peers."[6]

The impact of gun violence extends beyond direct victims. In one recent study, a third of all Black adults (31 percent) reported witnessing someone being shot.[7] A third of Black adults (34 percent) said they have a family member who was killed by a gun, twice the percentage of white adults who said the same (17 percent).[8] One-third of Black adults (32 percent) said they worry either "every day," or "almost every day" that they or one of their loved ones will be a victim of gun violence, compared to one in ten white adults.[9] And one in five Black adults (20 percent) feel like gun-related crimes, deaths, and injuries constantly threaten their local community—which is more than double the percentage of white adults who say the same (8 percent).[10]

Some of the effects of gun violence are visible. Some are much harder to see. People who live in neighborhoods with high levels of violence, regardless of whether they are personally impacted, often deal with chronic stress, impaired cognitive function, and poor health outcomes, due, in part, to the persistent experience of trauma.[11] What that means is that when someone is shot, it doesn't just affect that individual person. It affects entire families—and communities. And children who grow up in neighborhoods where violence is prevalent are more likely to experience chronic stress, academic underachievement, and mental health problems—which of course impedes their paths to economic mobility.

What We've Learned

Gun violence is a multifaceted problem, and the ways of addressing it are multifaceted, too. As the National Institute for Criminal Justice Reform (NICJR) has described, violence reduction occurs in a continuum from **prevention**—the earlier supports for children and youth; to **intervention**—the short-term interruption of immediate violence; to **community transformation**—the long-term efforts to change conditions in neighborhoods of concentrated poverty to lead to greater stability, economic opportunity, and hope.[12]

From Ballmer Group's early days, we understood that addressing community violence is essential to creating the conditions necessary for economic mobility. We fund efforts all along the continuum of prevention to intervention to community transformation—but it was clear that we needed to address the immediate reality of gun violence. So, we supported gang prevention and intervention efforts in LA,[13,14] hospital-based violence intervention in Detroit,[15,16] and a collaborative effort to reduce gun violence, as well as street outreach and employment training, in Chicago.[17,18] From those investments, we've learned three important lessons:

1.   The number of people who are most at risk of being victims or perpetrators of gun violence is definable, and small—and therefore addressable.
2.   Efforts to reach, redirect, and support individuals at highest risk of gun violence are most effective when they're provided by trusted individuals or "credible messengers" who share similar life experiences.
3.   There are proven, effective approaches to violence reduction, but most have limited reach.

Based on our learnings, we became convinced that reducing gun violence in low-income, urban communities *is* achievable—and that it requires a comprehensive, strategic approach that uses data to identify and provide intensive services to individuals who are at highest risk, and centers the experiences of communities who are facing the harm we are trying to prevent. We also realized that in order to make a larger impact, we needed to expand our work and support efforts in multiple places. In 2015, half of all gun homicides took place in just 127 cities.[19] We may not be able to get to all 127—but we wanted to try to make a difference in as many as possible.

Community Violence Intervention (CVI)

At the same time, there was growing understanding and support from local, state, and even the federal government[20,21,22] about the important role of what is now called community violence intervention (CVI) in keeping communities safe. There are different strategies or specialties within CVI.[23] The violence interruption and street outreach work we funded in LA, to mediate conflicts and stop retaliatory shootings, is one form of CVI. So is the work we funded in Detroit, which reaches high-risk individuals in the hospital, after they've been shot, to offer trauma-informed, community-based care; and the life coaching and workforce development we supported in Chicago. Other models connect high-risk individuals to networks of wraparound services; or enroll them in courses that include mentoring and modest stipends; or provide trauma-informed cognitive behavioral therapy. Depending on the specific needs of a neighborhood, or city, different mixes of approaches might be needed. But we hadn't found an effort that supported all these things in a more coordinated way.

Then, in 2020 and 2021, we began talking to a group of leaders who proposed doing just that: coordinating their work and developing an ecosystem approach. A CVI ecosystem, sometimes driven by city leadership and sometimes managed externally in partnership with the city, connects a city's violence prevention infrastructure—including community-based organizations, offices of neighborhood safety, and public health departments that often work separately—in order to implement a comprehensive strategy that addresses violence dynamics.[24] This ecosystem often parallels—and sometimes works with—law enforcement, reaching people and communities that police cannot.

In early 2022, Ballmer Group contributed $20 million to this innovative approach by investing in four Training and Technical Assistance organizations that reflect the range of CVI strategies—the Health Alliance for Violence Intervention, the Community Based Public Safety Collective, Cities United, and the National Institute for Criminal Justice Reform—to jointly establish community-based solutions to gun violence.[25] This is the first time that all four organizations—now known collectively as the Coalition to Advance Public Safety (CAPS)—have been funded to bring their respective violence reduction strategies together.[26] The groups are collaborating to reduce community gun violence in twelve U.S. cities by developing CVI ecosystems and providing training and technical assistance, as well as ongoing support for CVI organizations on the ground. Other partners—most notably the Charles and Lynn Schusterman Family Philanthropies and Blue Meridian Partners—have joined us in supporting this effort. With the resources to scale up their work and build a strategic infrastructure, we believe that these four organizations—whose leaders all have their own experiences with violence in their neighborhoods or families—can catalyze a significant reduction in gun violence throughout the country.[27]

We already know that CVI works. In Oakland, gun violence has dropped by 50 percent since the city implemented Oakland Ceasefire.[28] Newark, New Jersey, experienced a drop from 3,200 violent crimes to 1,500 in five years after adopting the street out-reach and intervention approaches of the Newark Community Street Team.[29] Baltimore, Chicago, New York City, and Philadelphia have each seen a more than 30 percent reduction in shootings and killings when deploying the Cure Violence model.[30] Over the course of four years, in three Connecticut cities where 70 percent of the state's gun homicides occurred, gun homicides declined by 50 percent after Project Longevity.[31] In LA, the city's Gang Reduction and Youth Development program resulted in significantly fewer retaliations[32]—saving both public costs and, more importantly, lives; and in Chicago, both Chicago CRED and READI Chicago have been shown to be effective by multiple recent studies.[33,34,35] These results are all encouraging, but more research and evaluation is needed. And we're also excited to learn whether coordinating efforts through CAPS—bringing multiple strategies to bear

in a single place—can move the numbers even further. With growing evidence about the effectiveness of CVI, there's a strong case
for expanded public funding—which is why we also recently supported the Community Justice Action Fund, which is advocating
for greater investment in CVI at the city, state, and federal levels.[36]

Time to Act

On the court, the LA Clippers always work to compete at the
highest level. I often talk about the shot clock: every twenty-four
seconds, our fans expect us to score a basket. We don't have the
luxury of waiting until conditions are perfect—we have to work

with what's in front of us, and every moment counts. The same is true off the court: we have to act now.

Governing an NBA team is about more than just winning; it's also about creating a positive impact and getting wins in the community. Sports teams are community assets, and through the NBA, we have a unique platform through which we can try and help change the world for the better. I can't say I know what it's like to grow up in poverty, or to experience gun violence in my neighborhood. But there are people who have the experiences and the expertise to help. And there's one thing I do know: too many people have been locked out of opportunity for too long.

I am committed to creating paths for more upward mobility in the U.S., and to ensuring that communities are leading the way in keeping our children and families safe. It's why Ballmer Group exists. It's why I serve on the board of the National Basketball Social Justice Coalition. I care deeply about young people having access to the opportunities they deserve—and overcoming the obstacles that hold them back. It's not acceptable to me that so many young people—especially young Black men—have been deprived of education, of opportunity, of hope. It's not acceptable that so many lives have been lost, futures cut short, and families and communities torn apart because of gun violence. This is why we do our work—because it's right, and because we must.

2

DOING THE WORK

J. B. BICKERSTAFF

Head Coach, Detroit Pistons
Board, National Basketball Social Justice Coalition

My Father

My dad was a pioneer, not just on the basketball court, but also in the way he created opportunities for Black and poor people throughout his adult life. His success in both arenas did not come easily. Born in 1944, he grew up in Benham, Kentucky, a small town near the Virginia and Tennessee border decimated of its economic vitality by the Great Depression. His house had no plumbing and no phone. Much of the town was openly racist. My dad could not eat or drink with white people; he had to move to the back of the bus after boarding; his basketball team traveled forty-four miles round-trip to practice at the "colored" school, Harlan Rosewald, even though the town had a basketball facility within walking distance.[1] That inhumane arrangement persisted until 1959 or 1960. My dad dreamed big, but always thought that he would likely end up working in the coal mines like his grandfather who raised him and ended up with black lung disease. Instead, my dad ended up an NBA basketball coach.

In the mid-1960s, things finally improved for him. He moved to San Diego, where he played basketball for the University of San Diego Toreros. Graduating in 1966, he went to play for the Harlem Globetrotters for a time and eventually moved back to San Diego to marry my mom and start his coaching career as an assistant at USD. He was one of just a handful of Black coaches in college basketball. The rest, as they say, is history: my father became head coach of the Seattle SuperSonics; president and general manager of the Denver Nuggets; head coach of the Washington Bullets; head coach and general manager of the Charlotte Bobcats; assistant coach and interim coach of the Los Angeles Lakers; and assistant coach of the Cleveland Cavaliers.

I may never be able to fully grasp the challenges my father faced; and maybe I'll never know the full toll such obstacles must have taken on him. But what I do know is that he, miraculously, took those experiences and used them as fuel for a desire to shatter barriers throughout his entire life. And in doing so, he modeled several key values for me every day of my life—values I still hold dear today. He had a relentless work ethic. If you deserved it, he was loyal. He had grit. That combination allowed him to succeed in a world that, for much of his early life, seemed only to want to see him fail.

Despite all his accomplishments, my father remained cleareyed about how racism impacted his life and continues to impact so many. And he has never forgotten the equally damaging effects of economic inequality. The town my dad grew up in struggled, like so many coal towns in Appalachia, which spans Kentucky, Virginia, and Tennessee. President Lyndon B. Johnson referred to it as "a world apart." In the 1960s, one-third of families there lived in poverty, unemployment rates were above the national average, and in Appalachian Kentucky, over 20 percent of adults had less than five years of schooling.[2] It's not because people didn't want to lead better lives. It's just that they had no opportunity to do so. Today, the decline in our country's reliance on coal production has only worsened the economic strain.

Picking Up the Baton

I had opportunities, in large part, thanks to my dad. But he didn't just fight for me. Whenever he could, he worked hard to make sure all people could break through barriers and improve their station in life—especially people of color and those from poor communities. He knew what the struggle looked like, and he wanted to eliminate it wherever possible.

So when people ask me why I engage in social justice work when I could just stick to basketball, the answer is simple: my parents, Bernie and Eugenia Bickerstaff.

Of course, many of the battles I am fighting today look a little different—although sadly, many are the same. I am especially committed to breaking down the stigma Black men often feel about seeking mental health treatment. When you consider, for example, the profound emotional and psychological impact that news of incidents of police violence has on Black communities, it quickly becomes clear how mental health is tied to racial justice.[3] In fact, Black men and boys who are racially profiled by law enforcement are at increased risk of anxiety and post-traumatic stress symptoms afterward.[4] Research shows Black men who have experienced trauma are significantly less likely to seek help, even when that trauma is serious. Yet so many of us suffer from it. Sixty-two percent of Black men have directly experienced a traumatic event, 72 percent have witnessed[5] a traumatic event, and 59 percent have a friend or family member who has lived through one.[6] Trauma has genuine effects if not treated. It can lead to post-traumatic stress, persistent fatigue, sleep disorders, and massive anxiety.[7]

To start to address this problem, along with the Cleveland Cavaliers and the NAACP Cleveland Branch, we started a series: "Black Men: It's Time to Talk."[8] I want people to feel like they can acknowledge what it is that is causing them anxiety or depression, and then begin to address it and make it better. Nothing good comes from bottling up your problems—and it's now well-known that this behavior can worsen our mental health, severely compromise our physical health, and negatively impact our relationships.[9] In the game of basketball, seasoned players are willing and expected to ask each other for help guarding an opponent on defense. It should be no different when they are struggling.

Another important battle still going on is voting. We need to make it easier for people to vote. Many officials are trying to do the opposite, enacting strict voter identification laws and even making it illegal to give food to voters waiting in line.[10] In Cleveland, we wanted to make it easier. And we wanted people to be excited to do it. In 2020, we opened Rocket Mortgage FieldHouse as a voter registration site[11] and opened it as a polling site on election day.[12] I know that the Cavaliers will continue finding ways to bolster civic engagement during the 2024 general election.[13]

Deeper Learning

In order to eradicate racism and poverty, those of us with platforms need to go beyond what know; we need to learn more so we can do more in the communities where we live, work, and play. And there was plenty to do in Cleveland. It is a strong city with rich cultural heritage that Clevelanders are rightly proud of. And it is important to me to continue my education on justice issues impacting the city and state so that I could be part of this community's progress.

I learned that we need to focus on our communities as a whole and invest in education, mental health services, substance use services, housing, employment, and job training. These types of investments are proven community-based approaches to public safety because they address the root causes of violence *before* it happens.[14] If we use these services better, we can shift the burden from police to other trained and licensed professionals. That would be a major step toward a healthier, more stable, and economically secure community.

I was encouraged to learn that Cleveland is embracing community-based strategies for public safety. In 2020, the city invested in a co-response pilot program that relies on social workers to respond to crisis. Instead of sending traditional police to handle mental health crises, two-person teams (one social worker and one officer trained in crisis response) are deployed to deescalate the situation, connect the involved people to social support services, or take them to an emergency room for treatment. This is a much safer, more humane, and just alternative to arresting and jailing somebody in distress. While the teams have only been able to respond to a small percentage of calls,[15] with $5 million in federal aid, the city plans to double the program's staff.

Finally, I've learned the poverty rate is 2.5 times the national average.[16] A heartbreaking 45.5 percent of children in Cleveland are growing up in poverty, and more than half of those kids are under five years old. This disproportionately impacts the Black community: in Cuyahoga County, Black residents have a 27.2 percent poverty rate—three times that of white residents in the exact same place.[17] All the many social challenges we have are only made worse by the crushing weight of poverty—the very same thing my father experienced, overcame, and vowed to continue fighting.

We have more work to do.

Commitment

I am especially proud of how the NBA family has taken on race and equity issues, including creation of the National Basketball Social Justice Coalition. We exist thanks to the legacy of the Cleveland Summit—which the Cavaliers and the Coalition commemorated with a historical marker in 2022—where Muhammad Ali, Kareem Abdul-Jabbar, Jim Brown, Bill Russell, and Carl Stokes, among other notable Black athletes, gathered in support of Ali's protest of the Vietnam War. I am proud to have joined the Board of Directors of this new venture.

The Social Justice Coalition and the National Basketball Coaches Association's committee Coaches for Racial Justice,[18] which I am also a part of, started after we all watched the video of George Floyd being killed on camera. Like the many millions who saw the same horror, we were disgusted. We also felt intense despair, because many of us had then (and since) witnessed so many other police-involved fatalities. After each one, people would take to the streets and demand change, only for nothing meaningful to happen. Elected officials would express thoughts and prayers. Maybe a police department would fire an offending police officer; but mostly, we would all just wait and hold our collective breath until the next shooting. Many of us across the NBA community felt like we kept revisiting the same issue, only to have it fade into the background. What we knew we couldn't do was stand by and do nothing.

We knew we had something at the NBA that others don't: the ability to keep these issues in the forefront of the public's mind. People who protest can't take to the streets every single day. And most people who make up movements have other jobs, or school, or family obligations. Even if they could, eventually, the media would stop paying attention.

The media shows up every single night for our games. Reporters show up at our practices. Fans watch and read our social media accounts. They read blogs about what we say. They tune in and they show up. We also have an audience that cares about social justice the same way that we do. In the last few decades, we at the NBA have always been able to use our individual platforms to talk about issues that are important to us. It's easy to tune out one person or to label him as an outlier; but when so many in our league unite around the same message and keep talking about issues that matter to us, we become impossible to ignore.

I feel a responsibility to be part of the discussion—to stand for racial justice and equity. But everyone in this country should. I believe that the reason we haven't made as much progress is that we have allowed people to be neutral and stand on the sidelines. Racism is not just a Black problem; it impacts all of us and prevents all of us from reaching our highest collective potential. The Coaches for Racial Justice committee—which is led by Lloyd Pierce and includes Gregg Popovich, Steve Kerr, David Fizdale,

Stan Van Gundy, Doc Rivers, Quin Snyder, and me—is focused on change at the national and local levels. The committee has been advised by Campaign Zero, Color of Change, the Equal Justice Initiative, and My Brother's Keeper—organizations that work on civil rights advocacy, criminal justice reform, and economic opportunities for communities of color. Together we have both encouraged people to both get out of their comfort zone and become active in the fight for racial equity and social justice.[19]

Doing this work alongside peers and allies is even more important now than it ever has been before. Every day, something terrible seems to happen in this world. In 2020, as we were being bombarded with news of police violence, we were already dealing with an unprecedented pandemic and at the beginning of a recession that pushed many who were already struggling into unemployment. Things have felt consistently hard for so many for too long. It's easy, for people with more power and means to lose focus or look away. But we can't afford to let up. And that means we must continue to find the right places to talk about issues that matter and bring more people into the fold with us.

To those who are thinking about joining us: now is the time. Doing social justice work can seem daunting, especially when there is so much casual vitriol between people with different views. But I promise you, with a little courage, it's easier than it looks. It's certainly easier than what my dad and his generation experienced. If we are each willing to listen, to learn, and to act, we can honor the legacy they left and continue on the journey to creating a more equitable future—together.

3

The Question That Drives Me

MALCOLM M. BROGDON

Point Guard, Washington Wizards
Founder, Brogdon Family Foundation

The Question

"Now what?"

I will never forget my mother's question as I left one of my first protests: a demonstration in Atlanta in the aftermath of George Floyd's murder.

While proud that I attended, she didn't let me take even a momentary pause afterward. I know my mom. With her question, she intended to unsettle me: stirring the lessons of my family's past to motivate me in charting a path forward. A path that might contribute to real progress in America.

Fighting for change is in my blood. My parents named me after Malcolm X, the visionary civil rights leader who advocated for Black power, pride, and dignity. One of his core beliefs was that African Americans had been systematically oppressed and marginalized due to institutional racism, but that through self-reliance they could rise above. He stressed the importance of education, saying "If you don't have education, then you have no future."

My parents raised me according to these principles, taking every opportunity to impart a lesson. When I was little, they moved our family out of a middle-class neighborhood into Sweet Auburn Historic District, a neighborhood in inner-city Atlanta. An unusual, but deliberate decision, our home was now just one block from Dr. Martin Luther King Jr.'s home on Auburn Avenue and within walking distance of the MLK Center for Nonviolent Social Change. From the 1890s to the 1930s, Auburn Avenue had been the commercial center of Black Atlanta.[1] In 1956, *Fortune* magazine named it "the richest Negro street in America," home to one of the largest concentrations of African American businesses in the United States.

But, by the time we moved in 2001, Sweet Auburn was a struggling, low-income neighborhood.[2] Like too many other inner-city areas, our neighborhood was a casualty of disinvestment, homelessness, and crime, worsened by the construction of the Downtown Connector freeway, which split the neighborhood in two. Later, at different points, Sweet Auburn was deemed one of "America's 11 Most Endangered Historic Places"[3] and one of the "Places of Peril."[4]

My two brothers and I played basketball on a court just behind our backyard. The people we would see around the court included some who were using drugs and battling addiction. Many of those folks became our friends; they were an integral part of our community growing up. Where many parents may have feared for their children's safety in a neighborhood that had suffered like Sweet Auburn, my parents saw an opportunity to ensure that we understood that all people have dignity regardless of circumstance and that we were clear-eyed about what many Americans experienced in their daily lives while trying to make ends meet. Thanks to my parents, even before I could articulate it clearly, I was well versed in the real-world impacts of racism and our country's systemic failures.

Living History

As I grew, I spent a lot of time at Dr. King's alma mater, Morehouse College, an HBCU (Historically Black College and University), where my mother, Dr. Jann Adams—now associate vice president for advancement and leadership initiatives—worked. Established two years after the Civil War to educate those newly freed from slavery, Morehouse was founded by Rev. William Jefferson White, the son of enslaved people, with the encouragement of Rev. Richard C. Coulter, who had previously been enslaved, and Rev. Edmund Turney.

Often we talk about the civil rights movement of the 1950s and '60s as if it happened so long ago. The photos and footage of the time are largely black-and-white and create a kind of optical illusion of distance. But those days are still within living memory. This year, Bernice King, Dr. King's daughter, wrote that the reason she shared only color photos of her father on MLK Day was to remind people that it wasn't that long ago that discrimination and racist, unjust laws and policies were the law of the land; business as usual.[5]

My mother would tell us stories about the Ku Klux Klan violently terrorizing Black people throughout the South with impunity—a far cry from what our life was like growing up in Georgia.

And then there was my grandfather, a vibrant reminder of the civil rights movement. An icon.

John Hurst Adams, or "Poppo" as we called him, grew up in South Carolina. His father, my great-grandfather Eugene Avery Adams, was an AME Church minister in South Carolina, as well as the president of his local NAACP chapter, and protested police brutality in his time. This meant my family was frequently in the crosshairs of the Klan, and Poppo would sometimes wake up to crosses burning on his family's lawn.

In his twenties, my grandfather was called to fight for more. In 1956, he became president of Paul Quinn College, an AME-affiliated HBCU in Waco, Texas, which was well-known as "a very segregated country town."[6] His welcome gift included yet another burning cross on the lawn of his new home, courtesy of the KKK.[7] But he remained steadfast and unshaken. While president, he introduced students to activism, personally driving many of them to hear his friend Dr. King speak. Although reliant on support from white donors to ensure Paul Quinn's sustainability, when asked to intervene in student-led sit-ins protesting the segregation of Waco's businesses, he refused, ultimately leading city leaders to desegregate the community themselves.[8]

In the 1960s, my grandfather counseled AME members across the country—including as pastor of Seattle's First AME Church, the oldest in the state of Washington.[9] It was in Seattle that he became one of the most visible civil rights leaders and strategists. In 1965, after a Black man was killed by Seattle police, he organized "freedom patrols"—groups of community members to monitor and follow police officers to prevent abuse and ensure fair treatment.[10] He was often vocal about widespread housing segregation, and he marched regularly with Dr. King, including attending the fifty-four-mile Selma-to-Montgomery civil rights march in 1965.

Between 1968 and 1972, he led a church in Los Angeles and developed an education program focused on teaching Black children Black history and pride.[11] He helped to create the Congress of National Black Churches (now the Conference of National Black Churches),[12] with a goal of elevating Black Christian voices and concerns given his experiences with the ongoing reluctance of white Christians to challenge injustice.

In 1992, the year I was born, my grandfather returned home to the South. Starting in 1994, he was one of the strongest voices calling for removing the Confederate flag from the South Carolina State House, declaring "that house on Main Street belongs as much to me as it does to anybody else in the state."[13] The flag was removed from the dome in 2000—but remained on the grounds.[14] He also fought for Dr. King's birthday to be recognized as a state holiday in South Carolina—the last state in the nation to do so.[15]

Not too many people get to say they learned at the feet of a civil rights hero. A true giant among men. My grandfather exemplified how to live a courageous life. He used his influence to collaborate with other civil rights leaders and helped build strategies for how they would fight for and win real progress.

He stood up for justice his entire life. He never stayed still and never stayed silent. And he did it while facing extraordinary odds. My grandfather was, and is, a permanent reminder of what our community fought for; and his memory is an inspiration for the fights we continue today.

Oscar

A sports fan and an athlete in his own right, every so often Poppo would call us to debate who was the greatest basketball player of all time. His answer was always the same: Oscar "The Big O" Robertson. To my grandfather, this debate was never just about career stats, points per game, rebounds, assists, winningest record, All-Star appearances, NBA titles, or player awards. Don't get me wrong, the Big O was what people would call a "triple-double machine" and a top-scoring guard who became a twelve-time All-Star, an MVP, and an NBA champion.

But Robertson's most significant accomplishments happened off the court. And he often stood alone in these battles. As president of the National Basketball Players Association, he was the first African American president of any national sports or entertainment labor union. He was also the NBPA's longest-serving president. He led the union at a time when players had very few rights and protections. Back then, players did not have access to a doctor when they got hurt, were limited to eight dollars a day for meal money, and very few had contracts that were guaranteed. There was no such thing as free agency—meaning that team owners maintained perpetual employment rights over players. In other words, your employer could end your contract with a team for the most trivial of reasons and prevent you from playing professional basketball again. At that time, players who joined the NBPA were not protected against retaliation by coaches.[16]

To rectify these injustices, in 1970, under Robertson's leadership, the NBPA filed the first antitrust lawsuit in professional sports. The class-action suit that players won resulted in improved salaries and working conditions, and "the right for each player to earn according to his ability in a fair market."[17] When players won the case, team owners in turn attempted to get Congress to grant a special antitrust exemption so that they could again limit players' power. Again Robertson raised his voice, testifying before Congress and securing a settlement that resulted in what is now known as the "Oscar Robertson Rule," which allowed players to change teams without the original team retaining contract rights.[18] Given another opportunity, Robertson said, even with the professional and personal risk, he'd do it all again to ensure that "basketball players, athletes and African Americans should be treated as any other person in American life."[19]

Our Icons

This generation of professional athletes—and those that will follow—are lucky to have groundbreaking predecessors like Oscar who have shown us what it looks like to stand up for your beliefs. Athletes whose quest for justice was no barrier to excellence in their craft. Sportsman and activist. Two sides of the same coin.

There was Muhammad Ali, one of my biggest heroes. A departure from athletes whose activism had up to that point mostly taken a quiet, heads-down approach, working to racially integrate professional sports, Ali was brash, outspoken, unapologetically Black, and proud. He was the world heavyweight champion by 1964, at just twenty-two years old. His story is now the stuff of legend: when he refused to be drafted into the U.S. Army in 1967 citing his religious beliefs and opposition to the Vietnam War, he was stripped of his title, banned from boxing from the ages of twenty-five through twenty-eight (his prime athletic years), and threatened with a five-year prison sentence.[20] Ali's fights out-side the ring extended to the developing world, including parts of the world where U.S. policymakers preferred not to engage.[21] Dedicated to combating injustice everywhere, he later traveled to Afghanistan and North Korea on goodwill missions; to Cuba, where he delivered medical supplies to local hospitals and clinics; to Iraq to secure the release of fifteen hostages; and to South Africa when apartheid ended.[22] Through his actions, Ali showed how much he cared for all people, no matter their race, ethnicity, or nationality.

There was Bill Russell, giant of the Boston Celtics in the 1950s and '60s. Like my grandfather, he marched with Dr. King at the height of the civil rights movement. At the Cleveland Summit of 1967, he rallied with eleven other prominent Black athletes, in-cluding Kareem Abdul-Jabbar, to support Muhammad Ali in the aftermath of his Vietnam War protest. Russell led the very first boycott of an NBA game after his teammates were refused ser-vice at their hotel's café in Kentucky before a preseason exhibi-tion game because of the color of their skin. Russell stressed the importance of taking action on civil rights issues, saying, "we've got to show our disapproval of this kind of treatment or else the status quo will prevail."[23] During his thirteen seasons with the Celtics, he won eleven NBA titles, more than any other player in history. Decades later, like Ali, he was awarded the Presidential Medal of Freedom, the highest civilian award in the U.S., for his humanitarian activism.[24]

And there was Arthur Ashe, a tennis player in the 1960s and '70s who won three Grand Slam singles titles and two in doubles. He is still the only Black man to ever win singles titles at Wimble-don, the U.S. Open, and the Australian Open.[25] Repeatedly denied visas to travel to South Africa to compete in matches, he used his influence to call out systemic racial segregation and apartheid in the country. He lobbied for the U.S. government to impose sanctions and was even arrested protesting at the South African Embassy in Washington, DC.[26] Later, after contracting HIV through a blood transfusion, he worked to raise awareness of the disease and reduce the stigma associated with it.[27] He, too, received a Presidential Medal of Freedom after his death.

The Work Continues

As my family history makes clear, we are, sadly, still fighting many of the same battles that our grandparents and great-grandparents fought. In 2015, white supremacist Dylann Roof entered Emanuel AME Church in Charleston, South Carolina, and murdered nine Black people who were just trying to worship. It was only then that legislators finally removed the Confederate flag from South Carolina state grounds. In 2017, white nationalists marched on Charlottesville, home of the University of Virginia, where I earned my degrees, to protest the removal of a statue of Confederate general Robert E. Lee. In 2020, we bore witness to one Black death after another at the hands of police.

We are still fighting for a fair criminal justice system. We are still fighting for our communities to be safe. We are still fighting for equal opportunity. And now we are fighting to make sure the next generation still has access to the lessons of the past and can learn the lessons I learned from my grandfather.

The work is not done.

"Now what?"

Even as I carry the spirit of my grandfather and other civil rights heroes with me, I recognize that my path is my own. My platform is my own.

Criminal justice reform is one of my areas of focus because it affects people who look like me the most, people in my community, people I am around every day. Many athletes are drawn to speaking against injustice because, when they are not on the court or on the field, they are part of communities experiencing the injustice and inequity that has led to the intimidation, abuse, and murder of people who look like them.

With this in mind, I advocated for Raise the Age in Massachusetts while I played for the Boston Celtics.[28] Our current system, which sends older teens into the adult system, has resulted in the population of justice-involved eighteen- to twenty-year-olds having the worst outcomes and the worst recidivism rates. Exposed to toxic environments like adult jails and prisons, 75 percent of young people end up being rearrested and 50 percent end up being reconvicted. We are not rehabilitating them. We are not serving them. That is injustice.

The Raise the Age bill would raise the age of juvenile court supervision from eighteen to twenty-one. The young people in juvenile systems end up with better outcomes than those pushed into the adult system because they are able to avoid adult criminal records that can haunt them their entire lives and severely impact their ability to get jobs, housing, food, and more. When young people are rehabilitated through appropriate interventions, they can go on to succeed and excel. When they succeed and excel, our communities are stronger.

Similar to the athletes who inspired me, I take a global view of justice. When I was eleven years old, my parents took me and my brothers on a three-week family service trip to Ghana, during which we worked at an outdoor daycare located next to a garbage dump, so that we, again, had the opportunity to be of service to others and better understand our own privileges. This trip and others later on were the inspiration when I launched the Brogdon Family Foundation, an endeavor to strategically channel impact. One of my greatest passions, we prioritize access to clean water through our Hoops4Humanity initiative, which has built up schools and freshwater wells in Tanzania and Kenya. We also champion access to education, through the John Hurst Adams Education Project, which has partnered with seven (and counting) Indianapolis-area schools on literacy initiatives and arranged tours of HBCU campuses for high school sophomores, juniors, and seniors.

The Question. Again.

"Now what?"

On August 26, 2020, the NBA season was in full swing. Only this was a season shortened by the global COVID-19 pandemic and being played by teams sequestered from the rest of the world in what became known as "The Bubble" in Orlando, Florida. That day, the Milwaukee Bucks, led by George Hill and Sterling Brown, did not play Game 5 of their first-round playoff series against the Orlando Magic, three days after a white police officer shot Jacob Blake in the back seven times in Wisconsin, and three months after George Floyd was murdered.

It was then–NBPA president Chris Paul who asked the same question my mom asked when I left the Floyd demonstration just a few months before. Paul had convened players in the Bubble that night to discuss the moment of national mourning and talk about how we as athletes could effect long-term change on racial justice. Players met with NBA leadership and team governors to outline several ways we thought the league could help advance racial justice and fight inequality that went beyond just raising awareness. They insisted on something that would last longer than any one player's career.

Ultimately, the league and its leaders pledged to establish a Social Justice Coalition of players, coaches, and governors. A coalition with representation from labor and management and without precedent in any professional sports league, which would advocate for justice-related public policy throughout the country. Thus the National Basketball Social Justice Coalition was created with a mission to pursue criminal justice, voting rights, policing, and community safety reforms.[29] During that period, the league also launched the NBA Foundation with a commitment of $300 million over ten years to support economic growth in the Black community.[30]

In addition to advocating for justice-related legislation and policy reforms, the Coalition supports stakeholders across the NBA community in their activism, no matter where they are in their journey. One of my first engagements with the Coalition was at Summer League 2022, when its leadership and staff hosted an intensive advocacy retreat for a small group of key individuals: members of the NBPA Executive Committee, including CJ McCollum (New Orleans Pelicans), Jaylen Brown (Boston Celtics), Grant Williams (Charlotte Hornets), and me; Head Coach Dwane Casey (formerly Detroit Pistons) and Assistant Coach Lloyd Pierce (Indiana Pacers); and executive John Thompson III (Washington Wizards). During that session, we began immersing ourselves in the legislative process, traditional and newer advocacy tools, considering how we could most effectively communicate with policymakers and partners, and planted seeds for our own sets of advocacy priorities.

Action

While the risks to life and limb may be lower today than the ones my grandfather and athletes in the 1960s faced, I recognize the reality that speaking up can still pose a risk to people who care about us and jeopardize our ability to provide for our families. But there is no shortage of ways to get involved in advocacy, whether you choose to wield a megaphone or march with the rest of the crowd. As someone with a master's degree in public policy, I am biased, but I especially believe that engaging in policy advocacy can and does lead to systemic, dramatic change in this world.

My grandfather taught me that *democracy* is an action word— to realize its promise, we must actively fight for justice and speak truth to power.

We can never stop pushing for the change we wish to see. We inherited the legacy of the giants who came before us and have a responsibility to carry their vision into the future.

"Now what?"

Do not be satisfied.

Find your path. Harness your power. Then keep going.

Keep protesting.

Keep advocating.

Keep working with your community to find solutions.

Keep pressuring your policymakers to fight for justice on your behalf.

Keep voting for people who will believe in justice for all.

Until justice rolls down like waters.

Until justice.

That's what.

4

TELLING MY STORY FOR GOOD

CARON BUTLER

Assistant Coach, Miami Heat
Founder, 3D Foundation
Trustee, Vera Institute of Justice
Author, *Tuff Juice: My Journey from
the Streets to the NBA*

From a Cell to a Championship

19,320 minutes. 322 hours. 23 hours a day, for two weeks. That's the amount of time I spent in solitary confinement. Locked in a prison cell the size of the average parking space. No sunlight or human interaction except the occasional strip search. Completely isolated from the world, you begin to lose track of time. Your sense of reality begins to slip away. You become anxious and paranoid. You are haunted by hallucinations and nightmares. You endure the humiliation of having every biological need—eating, sleeping, showering, urinating, defecating—happen within the same few square feet. Like an animal in a zoo. Imagine what that does to your spirit. Imagine what that does to a fifteen-year-old.

I grew up in a tough neighborhood in Racine, Wisconsin, a predominantly white city. Poverty, violence, and a lack of opportunities were the norm in my community. Drug dealers, able to access luxuries many of us could not, reigned supreme. In contrast, my mother worked two jobs, but it was never enough; every so often, we'd return home to find an eviction notice. We couldn't afford the place we had and we couldn't move somewhere safer. At a young age, I felt pressure to change our situation and help make ends meet. Given the realities of our neighborhood, I knew that if I was going to become anything, I was going to be the best drug dealer for my age. I honestly set that goal. And I achieved it; by the age of nine, I had learned how to use a gun; by eleven, I was selling cocaine on the south side of Racine; by thirteen, I had a $10,000 stash. By fifteen, I had a daughter on the way.

And then I was set up.

I was arrested after police found drugs—a quarter ounce of cocaine that wasn't mine—and a gun in my school locker. I was taken to an adult correctional facility. Two weeks later, after a fight with a member of a rival gang, I was in solitary confinement. Nothing I had seen up to that point—no stabbing, no shootout, no car chase, no murder—had prepared me for how defeated I felt in that situation. Completely alone and cut off from all human contact, I had plenty of time to reflect on my choices and whether I wanted to continue on this path. It was the lowest moment in my life, and it was the moment I decided that I'd had enough.

I spent two more months in the adult facility and was then taken to Ethan Allen School for Boys, a rough juvenile correctional facility in Delafield, Wisconsin, where I served twelve months. In all, I was locked up for fourteen months. I told myself that this time when I got out, I would enroll in school, get a job, and play basketball. Basketball was my ticket out.

I did everything I said I would do. I enrolled in Park High School. I started working at Burger King, making minimum wage. I started playing basketball at Bray Community Center. I transferred to a prep school, where, through basketball, I developed a relationship with living legend Coach Jim Calhoun of the University of Connecticut. When I received a scholarship to play at UConn, one of the most storied college basketball programs, it was a huge moment for my family, a sigh of relief. I'd made good on my promise. We had finally overcome.

The rest is history. With the same drive I'd had as a child to help provide for my family, I was drafted as the tenth overall pick in the 2002 draft, spent fourteen seasons in the NBA, became a two-time NBA All-Star, and became an NBA champion. Along the way, I had the honor of playing for the Miami Heat, Los Angeles Lakers, Washington Wizards, Dallas Mavericks, Los Angeles Clippers, Milwaukee Bucks, Oklahoma City Thunder, Detroit Pistons, and Sacramento Kings. And now I am an assistant coach for the Miami Heat.

Breaking the Cycle

It's tempting to not look back once you reach a certain level of success; but, almost thirty years later, I still think about how the system failed me and countless other young people like me. In Racine, an extremely segregated town, police used any excuse to lock Black kids up—loitering, sagging pants, being part of a group of five or more, riding a bicycle, general "suspicion." As a child, I was arrested fifteen times for minor infractions. At every turn, the system sought to degrade and dehumanize us. Starting with the police. They would jump us, stretch us out, and interrogate us in front of our neighbors for extended periods of time. Once at the detention facility, they would strip us, then tell us to bend over, spread our cheeks, and cough. Next, they would read out ridiculously trumped-up charges and begin calling us by number, rather than our names. In the courtroom, the district attorney, knowing we did not have the resources to protect ourselves from the system, would throw every charge at us— a widespread prosecutorial practice that has helped drive mass incarceration.[1]

Even when we were released back into the community, probation officers would come and pull us out of our classrooms and pat us down in front of the entire school. Instead of looking at us as kids, the system seemed intent on punishing us for our mistakes, pushing us to a point of no return. We were overpoliced, overcharged, and overprosecuted. Targeted by design. And it did not make any of us safer. At Bray Community Center, where I began playing organized basketball after being incarcerated, there's a picture of twenty-one Black boys, several of whom I used to run the streets with. They are all dead now.

I knew that once I broke the cycle of crime and violence in my own family, I would use my voice to help other people like me break the cycle too. I would advocate for a system that prioritizes rehabilitation, opportunity, counseling, and care over just punishment. I would push for a system that believes none of us are past redemption.

In an effort to do that, I have become comfortable with telling my story and the story of my community, releasing my autobiography, *Tuff Juice: My Journey from the Streets to the NBA*.[2] I have hosted a show, *1-on-1 with Caron Butler*, which is a series of candid conversations with civil rights leaders, NBA and WNBA players, legends, coaches, and executives to educate people on systemic racism, civic engagement, police brutality, and other issues impacting Black and brown communities.[3] I coauthored *Shot Clock* with Justin A. Reynolds, a young adult book series that touches on police brutality.[4] I founded the 3D Foundation, which, through instruction on fundamental basketball skills, supports youth development in the principles of determination, dedication, and discipline. I remain active in my community, speaking to young people about alternatives to violence and crime.

The Power of Rehabilitation

Many years after my time in juvenile and adult facilities, the system is still broken and, because of overly punitive and sometimes outright racist policies and practices, we lose gifted people to it each day. Every day, we hold 25,000 youth in juvenile facilities and the racial disparities persist. Kids of color are much more likely to end up in juvenile detention: in 2019, for example, the rate of white kids under eighteen placed in juvenile facilities was 72 per 100,000 youth; for Black kids, the rate was more than four times that at 315 per 100,000; for indigenous youth, 236 per 100,000; and for Latino/Hispanic kids, 92 per 100,000.[5] Nobody should be comfortable with those statistics.

In 2019, I joined the board of trustees at the Vera Institute of Justice. Vera focuses on drastically reducing the use of jails, prisons, and detention centers and championing a truly rehabilitative juvenile justice system—one that prioritizes support over punishment. Many who haven't been close to the system still wonder why prioritizing rehabilitation over punishment is crucial for the well-being of young people and for society.

We have answers backed by years of research.

First, rehabilitation offers young people the chance to break free from the cycle of delinquency they are almost always in and begin building fulfilling, productive lives. Many young people involved in the juvenile justice system have experienced significant trauma, abuse, or neglect, as well as resulting mental, emotional, and behavioral disorders, which can increase the risk of juvenile justice involvement.[6] Detention or incarceration doesn't address the underlying issues driving these kids' behavior, perpetuating cycles of crime.[7] Effective rehabilitation programs that provide access to counseling, education, job training, and supportive services have been shown to reduce recidivism rates among young people.[8]

Rehabilitation acknowledges that young people are still developing both cognitively and emotionally: they are still developing their ability to control impulses, weigh the consequences of their actions, consider other perspectives, and delay instant gratification.[9] As their brains develop, the vast majority of kids age out of lawbreaking and other risky behavior more commonly seen during adolescence.[10] Many rehabilitative interventions are tailored to meet the unique developmental needs of young people and have been found to promote positive youth development and resilience.[11]

I have learned about a range of rehabilitative alternatives that currently exist, including credible messenger programs, young advocate programs, restorative justice initiatives, wraparound services, cognitive behavioral therapy, and family-focused, multisystemic therapy.

Delivering Justice

Credible messenger mentoring programs hire community members with a history of involvement in the justice system to provide intensive support to kids and their families, setting goals related to their well-being and development. In New York City, for example, only 3 percent of participants in a credible messenger program were reconvicted within twelve months of completion.[12] Youth Advocate Programs (YAPs) assign trained advocates to work intensively with young people and their families and address underlying issues like trauma, substance abuse, and family conflict. One study on YAPs' impact showed that 86 percent of young people enrolled in a YAP remained arrest-free during their time in the program.[13]

Restorative justice interventions work with young people accused of serious offenses and provide an alternative to traditional court. This approach involves victims, and usually concludes with a conference where victims, youth who have been accused, and adults in their lives meet to discuss the harm caused and create a plan for the young person to "make things right." A study of the "Make It Right" restorative justice program in San Francisco found that restorative justice conferencing reduced participants' re-arrest rate by 33 percent in the year after enrollment, compared to peers who were prosecuted in court.[14] Victims who participated also reported a 90 percent satisfaction rate with the program.

Wraparound programs assign a care coordinator to develop individualized plans that provide a range of services to help those with serious emotional disturbances who may be facing serious delinquency charges. A study of a wraparound program in Milwaukee documented that, after the program, participating young people had shown substantial improvements in mental health and school attendance, and fewer placements into foster care or residential treatment programs. Also, just 14 percent of court-involved youth were rearrested, far lower than the 41 percent rearrest rate for those on probation who did not participate in wraparound.

In family-focused therapy models, therapists work closely with the vulnerable young person's entire family, engaging in frequent contact, to identify and address the factors that may lead them toward delinquent conduct. This model, used in many jurisdictions throughout the country,[15] has been assessed many times and been found to be highly effective.[16]

Finally, cognitive behavioral therapy connects those who are at extreme risk for future incarceration due to their proximity to neighborhood-based violence with therapy, education, employment, and other relevant services. These services can be delivered in an institutional or community-based setting and help participants recognize and change unhealthy thinking patterns and behaviors.[17]

In contrast to these highly effective alternatives, incarceration does not reduce delinquent behavior, undermines public safety, does lasting damage to physical and mental health, inhibits educational and career success, exposes kids to abuse, and further entrenches racial disparities. Young people who are released from correctional confinement experience high rates of rearrest, new adjudications in juvenile court or convictions in adult court, and reincarceration.[18]

Progress

There have been promising efforts to redress juvenile incarceration. Over the past five to ten years, many state and local justice systems have taken steps to redirect or "divert" more kids from juvenile court involvement.[19] Diversion means addressing delinquent conduct without involving the individual in the court system. It can happen at various points in the system: when authorities decide not to involve police or make an arrest (pre-arrest diversion); or when prosecutors decide that a young person referred to juvenile court should have their conduct addressed outside of the court (pre-court diversion).[20] In an effort to expand diversion opportunities, many states have raised the minimum age for offenses to be settled in delinquency court, taken steps to promote racial equity in diversion, prioritized alternatives that increase success of diverted youth, and improved data collection and sharing to improve diversion policies and programs.[21]

Many state legislatures are considering proposals to reduce the number of kids who become justice-involved, as well as prevent the harms of incarceration. Lawmakers have proposed bills to establish that a child has a right to an attorney before they can be interrogated by law enforcement; to raise the age at which children, and even young adults, may be tried in adult court; to end juvenile life without parole; to increase access to education in detention facilities; to improve the conditions of detention facilities; and to eliminate juvenile fines, fees, and costs.

Because of my experience, one of my main advocacy goals is to end solitary confinement in prisons. Far from being a last-resort measure, solitary confinement has become a first-resort control strategy in prisons and jails across the country. In addition to being used to address violence, people in prison are put into solitary for using profanity, having a mental illness, being gay or transgender, testing positive for drug use, reporting abuse by prison officials, or being children in need of "protection."[22] That is nothing short of inhumane.

In 2021, I advocated for Connecticut policymakers to pass and sign legislation that would require all incarcerated individuals be allowed at least 6.5 hours out of their cells daily and prevent the use of certain restraints. I spoke publicly about the trauma of solitary confinement and how people sometimes struggle to move past its psychological effects. As the lead organizer for the Stop Solitary CT campaign (part of the National Religious Campaign Against Torture) affirmed, people unfamiliar with the harms of our system often need someone they know to speak up on criminal justice issues because, without it, they often "have a hard time connecting with the humanity of incarcerated people."[23] Connecticut governor Ned Lamont ultimately approved a law that reduced the number of consecutive days a person can be kept in in isolation, increased required daily out-of-cell time for those in solitary to five hours, and put some restrictions on strip searches. But much more progress needs to be made.[24]

As of 2022, twenty-four states and the District of Columbia have enacted laws that limit or prohibit solitary confinement.[25] Twenty-eight states and the District of Columbia have banned life sentences without parole for kids under eighteen.[26] An incredible forty-six states have raised the age for adult court to eighteen years old.[27] But shockingly, no states guarantee the children can access an attorney while they are being interrogated by police.[28]

Worse, thirty-six states allow kids to be charged fees for "free" court-appointed lawyers.[29]

No Turning Back

Although there are many more harms to undo, we're seeing a return to tough-on-crime policies and rhetoric. After the emergence of the Movement for Black Lives and the largest racial justice reckoning in history, state legislatures are repealing justice-centered reforms. This is nothing new. After Reconstruction came Black Codes and lynchings. After Black Wall Street came the Tulsa Race Massacre.[30] After the gains of the civil rights movement, the government passed the 1968 Omnibus Crime Control and Safe

Streets Act, which gave outsize power to law enforcement. And so on.[31]

Whenever I see old arguments about public safety resurface, I remind myself that my own redemption would not be possible without adults who showed up for me against all odds: My mom, who moved our family from the south side of Racine to a calmer neighborhood in midtown so I wouldn't run with the same crowd. My family and friends who pooled their money together to give me the $5,500 tuition to attend that elite prep school. Officer Rick Geller, who, against recommendations from his fellow officers, chose to ask questions instead of making assumptions and saw me not as irredeemable but as a kid desperately trying to move on from a life of crime. They are the reason I never went back to that dark cell.

We can and must change the ineffective and unjust laws and practices that condemn our young people to endless cycles of system involvement. The truth is, these overly punitive, cruel policies have cost our country, our communities, and our children dearly. I will continue to relentlessly advocate for change. And I remain determined to be the kind of role model for kids today that I myself needed when I was growing up.

5

FOR OUR CHILDREN

TRE JONES

Guard, San Antonio Spurs
Board, National Basketball Social Justice Coalition

Uvalde, Texas
2022

After a year of remote learning due to the COVID-19 pandemic, Robb Elementary School students had returned to school. May 24, 2022, was supposed to be an easy day for students before they headed into summer break. Instead, a gunman with an AR-15 entered the school. The students and teachers followed their now-too-common active shooter training to a T, staying still and silent, crouching under desks and countertops, and keeping away from windows and doors. As bullets tore through their classmates' bodies, they tried to shush them, the words "quiet as a mouse"[1] and "act like you are asleep"[2] simultaneously running through their minds with previously inconceivable fear.

More than anything, they waited to be saved.[3] The gunman went back and forth between two classrooms, doubling down on the carnage he had already created. One of his victims, a teacher, later described the sensation of the bullets hitting his body as "hot lava."[4] Seventy-eight minutes later, another mass shooting in the United States had come to an end. The worst school shooting in Texas history. The third deadliest school shooting in U.S. history.

In total, nineteen students—all between the ages of nine and eleven—and two teachers were killed. Seventeen others were wounded.

They were just kids being kids, eighty-six miles from San Antonio, in a town called Uvalde.

Being a Father, Learning from My Mother

I love being a dad. My daughter, Zara, gives me the motivation to do anything. It has been amazing to see how she mirrors my behavior and language. Her existence puts everything into perspective. Unlike anyone else in my life, my daughter has given me the courage to push harder, to not take "no" for an answer.

By the end of this year, my house will be overflowing with girls. My wife, Maddy, is pregnant with twin girls, and we couldn't be more excited for two more blessings to teach and learn from. Family is the most important thing in my life, and my biggest dream is to raise all three daughters to value family as much as we do. I also hope that our kids find passion in something they love and pursue it. Beyond that, I hope and pray for a world that has fewer senseless acts of violence and injustice.

Even before you are aware of it, you start making plans for your children. You think about who they will be, what they will look like, what they will act like, what their interests will be. Where will they attend school? Will they play sports (especially basketball . . .)? Will they be creative? What kind of world will they grow up in?

Unfortunately, the excitement of parenting is often tempered by a scarier question: How will you keep your children safe from harm? Every parent thinks about this at some point—but that question seems to loom particularly large for Millennial and Gen Z parents raising kids today.

I have been blessed to have my mom, Debbie Jones, as an example of what a model parent looks like. Since she was young, she has faced every challenge with an undaunted, positive attitude. From the ages of four to fourteen, my mom wore a back brace as she battled pain and shortness of breath due to scoliosis. Somehow, she still participated and excelled in track, gymnastics, and softball and became a high school basketball star, ultimately leading her team to win the 1981 North Dakota Class A state championship. Despite a lifesaving surgery at sixteen to improve her lung capacity and reduce her pain, my mom couldn't play college basketball on the scholarship she received.

Even though my parents divorced when I was five years old, my mom did not give up on giving my brothers and me every ounce of her energy. She worked as a paralegal while simultaneously teaching us the fundamentals of basketball, football, baseball, and track in Apple Valley, Minnesota. She somehow made it to every practice, every game, and was always there for us no matter what. Thanks to those early lessons on strength and perseverance, and her constant support, my brother Tyus and I both went on to play at Duke; we are now living out our dreams in the NBA.

Five years ago, we received devastating news: our mom was diagnosed with breast cancer. Despite how scary this news is, she maintained that same courageous and positive attitude she'd had in high school, continuing to go to work and travel to support me and my brother at games. She woke up ready to fight every single day. She looked at the adversity she was facing as something to attack, something she could learn from and share with people later. Once again, she put others first.

We were overjoyed that my mom was declared cancer-free after just nine months. Her battle and how she showed up in those nine months taught me, yet again, that no matter what is thrown my way, how I approach it mentally is key. Above all, her experience and example helped crystallize that life is about so much more than basketball; it's about how you show up for your family and for your community when everything is on the line.

A National Epidemic

Horrific shootings like the one that took place in Uvalde are a reminder of just how fragile our communities are. Gun violence is rising across the nation—in big cities and in rural communities alike. Every day in the United States, 120 people are killed with guns and more than 200 are shot and wounded.[5] In the past five years, one in five Americans has been impacted by gun violence.[6]

Guns are the leading cause of death for children and teens in the U.S. Each year, nearly 4,000 children and teenagers are shot and killed, and 15,000 are shot and wounded—that's an average of 53 American children and teens every day.[7] When children and teenagers are killed with guns, 62 percent are homicides. In the

U.S., an estimated three million children witness a shooting each year.[8]

A reflection of the broader national picture, guns are the leading cause of death among children and teens in Texas. An average of 430 Texas children and teens die by guns every year, 58 percent of which are homicides. Between 2012 and 2021, gun deaths in Texas increased almost 50 percent, compared to 39 percent nationwide.[9] San Antonio ranked fourth in U.S. cities with the biggest increase in homicide rates in 2020. Austin, Fort Worth, and Houston also ranked in the top ten.[10] A truly alarming manifestation of everything being bigger in Texas.

We know that most gun violence doesn't happen at schools. Instead, it happens throughout communities—in homes, in workplaces, in places of worship, at the mall, at parks, in theaters, in concert venues, in neighborhoods, and at the grocery store. It's an epidemic. And it is most often concentrated in poor, segregated neighborhoods where there is little investment and few economic opportunities. Black and Latino communities are especially hard hit because of decades of underinvestment.

I did not know until recently that one shooting can result in three or more retaliatory shootings and that a small number of people, who drive most of the violence in these neighborhoods, are often caught in cycles of victimization and trauma, disconnected from work and school, and lack the community supports to divert them from violence and help them heal.[11]

Public Health and Violence

Even though the numbers are hard to look at, even though they show us that our families and communities are not being served by our traditional approach to preventing and addressing violence, and even though I am scared, I maintain a positive attitude and show up to fight every day for my daughters' futures. They are the main reason that I joined the board of the National Basketball Social Justice Coalition—so I could effect change and pursue safety for them and for all other kids like them.

Through my advocacy with the Coalition, I've begun my learning journey about community violence intervention (CVI) programs that are making a difference in our community safety challenges. CVI efforts focus on reducing homicides and shootings by establishing relationships with people at the center of gun violence in our communities—people at the highest risk of perpetuating violence, being a victim of violence, or both.[12]

Both evidence-based and community-informed, CVI programs are shown to reduce violent injuries and deaths. Neighborhoods in Baltimore, Chicago, New York City, Philadelphia, Sacramento, Boston, Chicago, Indianapolis, New Orleans, Oakland, and Stockton, California, have seen shootings and killings decline by 20–30 percent over the last several years as a result of CVI. These programs also save cities money across the medical and criminal justice systems.[13]

Statewide, there are new and ongoing efforts to address community violence. Recently, San Antonio became the latest Texas city, after Houston and Austin, to announce that it would use a public health framework to address violence.[14] That approach looks beyond traditional policing to find solutions that center the health of the individual and the community. The city has announced that it will focus on four areas that residents identified as priorities: crimes committed by youth, incidents involving guns, sexual assault, and domestic violence. By December 2025, the initiative calls for increasing the number of voluntarily surrendered guns to help address gun violence.[15] I, like many other parents, look forward to seeing concrete benchmarks unfold from the process.

Lasting Trauma

So, what happens to surviving parents and children after a shooting?

Well, I read that gun violence has changed the way Americans parent. In a survey, the *Washington Post* asked parents what they are doing about gun violence. One parent shared that she and her husband decided to move abroad to keep their ten-year-old and fourteen-year-old safe. Another mother said that because her daughter, now eighteen, was shot in 2019, she now asks the parents of her younger son's friends before a playdate or sleepover if they have guns and if they are secured and locked up.[16] Another parent said she always makes sure to say, "I love you," when she drops her kids off, always notes the exits wherever she is, and doesn't take her children to big outdoor parades or festivals anymore. Another parent, whose best friend was murdered in her neighborhood, says she has lost all sense of safety and has put the Life360 app on her children's phones and first-aid kits with QuikClot packages, a way to stop blood loss, in their backpacks.[17]

We hear similar stories in Uvalde, where the San Antonio Spurs organization has spent a lot of time with those impacted by the Robb Elementary School shooting. We felt that it was critical to show up for our neighbors in this time of unimaginable heartbreak and mourning. Six months after the shooting, our team held an open practice and fair at Uvalde High School in support of the students of Robb Elementary and their families. Our goal was to bring joy to the families and friends of the students and teachers who died, but we knew that the trauma and fear would remain. It was also a way to be an outlet for the kids who went through such horrific trauma, and an attempt to bring them joy through basketball.

One parent shared that her eldest daughter, a fourth grader, was across the hall from the two classrooms where the shooting took place. "Sudden hands, different people that look like the shooter—she did see the shooter through her classroom window. She is terrified by people who look like him, not that she judges, but people have (similar looks), and it's just scary."[18] Her daughter is terrified to leave home, but she was able to overcome her fear to be present that day. She met the legendary Manu Ginobili wearing a jersey from her uncle bearing the same name.[19]

As these stories reveal, the effect of gun violence does not end when a shooting ends. It has a lasting impact on survivors: people who have witnessed gun violence; have experienced intimate partner violence involving a gun; have been threatened with a gun; or have had a loved one shot, wounded, or killed, including by suicide.[20] One in three survivors reports living in fear and feeling unsafe, leading to trauma responses like hypervigilance, numbness, paranoia, anxiety, and depression.[21]

Trauma can even ripple beyond communities to those with similar identities (for example, immigrant, Black, Latino, woman, LGBTQ, etc.) and experiences with gun violence can result in collective or community trauma. People in these extended communities can also feel hopeless, numb, or hypervigilant. In fact, a national poll revealed that among parents who have children in school, an overwhelming 77 percent have said they were somewhat or very concerned about the threat of gun violence at their children's schools, and that the threat of gun violence weighed heavily on their children too; about 61 percent of parents surveyed said their children worried about gun violence at school "sometimes" or "a lot."[22]

Trauma-Informed Care

Left unaddressed, trauma from violence can lead to serious consequences for survivors, their families, and their communities, including unemployment and housing instability, addiction and other mental health challenges, and revictimization. When children witness violence, crime, and abuse, they are more likely to abuse drugs and alcohol; suffer from depression, anxiety, and post-traumatic stress disorder; resort to aggressive and violent behavior; and engage in criminal activity. If they live in neighborhoods where gun violence is common, they may spend less time outside being physically active. And they may have lower grades, test scores, and rates of high school graduation.[23]

Again, I believe there is some good news here. Expert analysis and data tell us that trauma-informed care support works and can prevent long-term negative consequences, transform lives, and keep communities safer.[24]

Informed by survivors of gun violence, the Alliance for Safety and Justice and Crime Survivors for Safety and Justice have several recommendations for how communities should approach trauma-informed care. They include investment in trauma recovery centers (a one-stop shop for comprehensive care, including mental health services and support navigating the justice system); increased funding for organizations on the front lines of responding to gun violence and providing peer-to-peer support to victims; expanding access to victims' compensation; and ensuring job and housing stability in the aftermath of violence.[25]

For children who witness gun violence, school-based programs that focus on social-emotional learning appear to reduce the negative effects of that exposure. Mentoring programs are also effective at improving academic performance and reducing youth violence.[26]

Outside of Spurs team events, I have developed a close relationship with the Tree City Spurs, a girls basketball team for ages nine to eleven in Uvalde's Parks & Recreation League. The team lost two players in the shooting and several other teammates sustained serious injuries. Throughout the season, I've hosted the girls and their families at the Spurs practice facility to try to uplift and encourage them.

One of the biggest takeaways from my conversations with the children and families is how important it is for them to experience an overwhelming amount of positivity. They deserve to feel like kids again, and to feel like the trauma they went through is not something that's forgotten by the community around them. They have also shared how important it is to them for those with platforms to continue to speak out and be active participants in the fight against gun violence. I've personally made sure to keep in contact with different parents and share on my social media platforms various events in Uvalde, as well as sharing with teammates, friends, and families.

Before the shooting, there weren't many trauma-informed services available in the area. Through my time with the girls, I became aware of the Children's Bereavement Center of South Texas, which offers grief support services, counseling, camps, and support groups for children and adults in the Uvalde community. They hosted a grief education camp that provided expressive arts activities such as painting, singing, songwriting, and a drumming circle.

Throughout the camp, children participated in exercises on how to acknowledge and accept the death of a loved one. They cried, laughed, and healed. I support the center because this is exactly the type of care our youth need in the aftermath of tragedy.

Keeping Our Kids Safe

I have come to understand that our kids are pretty strong. But, to be honest, I would prefer to live in a world where none of our kids are required to show that sort of strength. My daughters, the kids of Uvalde, and kids in every community throughout this country deserve to dream, to grow old, to build community, and to have children of their own someday if they want to. Most importantly, they deserve to live free of worry that they could be shot to death in a place like their own school.

We can act. We can prevent gun violence. We can heal trauma. We can keep our communities safe.

The San Antonio Spurs will continue to pour into the community of Uvalde, building upon the Sport for Healing Fund we formed in partnership with the Texas professional sports community; our investment in the creation of safe spaces to heal, including the Center for Comfort and Consults and an elementary school playground; our donations of equipment to youth basketball teams; our more than seven hundred volunteer hours; the more than $1 million in funds we've raised to support the community; and more.

The National Basketball Social Justice Coalition will continue to work to raise awareness about the national crisis of gun violence and the urgent need for federal, state, and local leaders to invest in the CVI programs and trauma-informed care that our communities desperately need.

I will continue to use my platform to amplify and support organizations that support communities grappling with gun violence. I will keep my commitment to my daughters to do everything I can to keep them and all other kids safe.

This essay is dedicated to the memories of Nevaeh, Jackie, Makenna, Jose, Ellie Gee, Uzi, Amerie, Xavier, Jayce, Tess, Maranda, Alithia, Annabell, Maite, Lexi, Layla, Jailah, Eliahna, Rojelio, Irma, Eva, and the countless other victims of gun violence.

FINDING THE PATH

CJ McCOLLUM

Guard, New Orleans Pelicans
President, National Basketball Players Association (NBPA)
Founder, CJ McCollum Dream Centers

Forks in the Road

There are many forks in the road in a kid's life—places where one right (or lucky) move can set you on a path to accomplish all your dreams; and one wrong move can set you on a very different road with potentially devastating consequences. Of course, the people who raise you and mentor you are critical in determining which path you take when those inevitable forks come around. Fortunately for me, I grew up surrounded by positive influences for most of my childhood in Canton, Ohio. Although my parents divorced when I was young, my father has played an active part in shaping the man I've become. He instilled in me the importance of good decision-making. And I have a loving and wonderful mother with whom I am very close; many basketball fans know that because I lived with her when I played for the Portland Trail Blazers. It's no secret that my mother valued and insisted on the importance of education, which is why throughout my time at Lehigh University, I took serious and intensive courses and majored in journalism.

I also saw the impact that making bad choices—even minor ones—could have on someone's future. As a kid, I watched several family members end up in prison. They were not and are not bad people; they just made some bad choices. And I'm not opposed to people facing consequences if they commit an offense. What has shocked me is that, all too often, the sentences handed down in our justice system don't fit what people are accused of having done. Worse was learning how callously the system treats people as soon as they first have contact with our justice apparatus. From policing, to prosecution, to prison, and beyond—throughout that cycle, for some reason, we suddenly stop treating people with the dignity and respect we all deserve as human beings. State by state, we make it extraordinarily difficult for people who have previously been incarcerated to get jobs, housing, occupational licenses, or go to college. It's like with one mistake—no matter how large or small—we decide someone is permanently less than the rest of us.

(In)justice in Louisiana

I knew and understood racial injustice from a young age, but very little could have prepared me for what I learned and saw when I came to New Orleans, Louisiana, to play for the Pelicans. The Big Easy is an incredible place. It is the birthplace of jazz and home to some of the best food in the world. It is amazingly diverse, with African, French, Spanish, Caribbean, and Native American cultures and histories all joining together. We host over 130 festivals—Mardi Gras, Jazz Fest, and Essence Festival, to name a few. Don't sleep on the state. The rest of Louisiana is full of natural beauty: you can watch sunsets over the bayou and make your way through swamps, marshes, rivers, and wetlands. People love to visit Louisiana. And I love living here.

But, in addition to the special cultural heritage, world-famous food, and iconic surroundings, what most people don't know is that the state and Orleans Parish are home to a devastating criminal justice machine that disproportionately harms Black people. For decades, people referred to Louisiana as the "world's prison capital" as it locks up a greater proportion of its residents than any other state besides Mississippi.[1] This fact alone underscores why we must stay committed to fighting the injustices we see right in front of us.

If I had to identify the worst part of the criminal justice system in this great state, it is how we treat children. It seems like we have all but given up on too many of our children from the time they are born here. A report released in 2020, for example, found that childhood trauma rates in Orleans Parish are "higher than [in] soldiers returning from war."[2] Incredibly, one in five children in New Orleans had witnessed a murder; four in ten had seen someone shot, stabbed, or beaten; and one in three had witnessed domestic violence. Of the five thousand children surveyed, more than half had someone close to them who was murdered.

The consequences of such exposure to trauma are well documented and devastating. Research shows that serious childhood trauma like this leads to adverse brain development, mental health problems, and, if untreated, an increase in the likelihood of committing crimes in the future.[3] One study found that child maltreatment, which can include neglect, doubles the likelihood that the child goes on to engage in criminal activity in the future.[4] When we fail to intervene with necessary treatments, it all but ensures that our kids will end up with bleak futures.

Treating Kids Like Kids

Sadly, the same report found that although Orleans Parish had a huge population of kids suffering from massive childhood trauma, they do not have the support that will help them heal. Kids who have lived in the traumatic equivalent of a war zone need interventions like cognitive behavioral therapy and many different types of counseling, and, of course, they need to feel safe—which means they need to be in a safe environment. The report details the acute need for deeper ties between the school system and health care agencies; it also notes how few of those responsible for overseeing kids are trained in trauma care. The report concluded: "As a result . . . they neither adequately meet the numbers of children in need nor do they provide a systematic process that can counter the symptoms of the traumatic experiences the children have suffered."[5]

Instead, Louisiana consistently ranks among the top ten states with the highest rates of juvenile incarceration, thanks especially to the zeal with which New Orleans has prosecuted kids over time.[6] For decades, state leaders have justified locking up children while ignoring the conditions they grew up in. Currently, Louisiana's juvenile incarceration rate is nearly double the national average.[7] Unsurprisingly, Black and brown kids suffer the most.

We have also sentenced our kids in some of the cruelest ways. Even as the use of juvenile life without parole (JLWOP) has decreased across the country, Louisiana has continued to use it: of all the JLWOP sentences doled out in the last decade, Louisiana and Georgia have issued half.[8] New Orleans has been a leader in sentencing kids to die in prison. At one point, only two counties— Philadelphia and Los Angeles—had sentenced more kids to life without parole.[9]

The state also leads the nation in sentencing kids to adult prison instead of keeping them in the juvenile system. In 2021, an astounding 7.2 percent of Louisiana's prison population was incarcerated for a crime committed before they turned eighteen. That's more than double the national average (3.1 percent). Eighty-three percent of those kids are Black.[10] Incredibly, between 2022 and 2023, the state incarcerated kids in Angola—a former slave plantation that now also happens to be the country's largest maximum-security adult prison.[11] When, after a year, a judge ordered those children removed from that awful facility, she documented how officials at the prison punished kids with solitary confinement for days, placed them in handcuffs, and denied them visits with their families. The conditions, she found, amounted to cruel and unusual punishment. As the lawyers on the case pointed out, almost all of the children held at Angola were Black boys.[12]

We are also out of step with the rest of the country on when we consider kids to be adults. In 2019, Louisiana finally raised the age of juvenile court jurisdiction from seventeen to eighteen. Only three other states at the time automatically sentenced seventeen-year-olds to adult court. In 2022, I wrote an op-ed in the New Orleans *Times-Picayune* calling for the law to be protected and remain on the books; I emphasized, as always, that "public safety and criminal justice reform are not mutually exclusive. They go hand in hand." But during this year's special legislative session focused on crime, the governor signed a bill to lower that age again, ensuring more kids will be incarcerated alongside adults.[13]

Incarcerating youth comes at a financial cost. One survey found that, on average, it costs $407.58 to lock up a child per day, $36,682 for three months, $74,364 for six months, and $148,767 for a year. Wouldn't it be better if we followed the science on rehabilitation and invested that money in getting kids counseling or treatment, perhaps a quality education, rather than a jail cell?[14]

Doing Our Part

To try to improve the way we treat our children in this parish and state, I have joined forces with the Louisiana Center for Children's Rights (LCCR). This organization works to fight laws and policies that systematically criminalize kids of color and poor kids, while representing those same young people in their individual criminal cases.[15] In response to my interest in learning more about the juvenile justice system and its impact on youth, LCCR took me to visit the New Orleans Juvenile Justice Intervention Center (JJIC) and Travis Hill School, the colocated high school that provides classes onsite for those kids. The school also provides medical and mental health support, individual treatment needs, and evidence-based treatment programming. It's the only place with such robust, holistic services in the state. Very few others even come close to that level of care.

The kids I met at the JJIC and Travis Hill School all made mistakes. But they were no less incredible as human beings and no less worthy of our care and concern. What they had to tell me as we talked was devastating. As we sat in a restorative justice circle, one student noted that they desperately needed mentors, saying, "We grew up knowing a lot of wrong. And if you are growing up and you don't know that wrong is wrong, that's what you do. You don't have a lot of people there in the community that are doctors, teachers. You do what you see."[16]

There is so much packed into those few sentences. Kids who grow up without positive role models are less likely to imagine possible futures for themselves; kids who grow up exposed to crime are less likely to see opportunities for growth. Few people give these kids a reason to feel safe or help them to see a different path. They experience trauma, get no mental health treatment, and then we are surprised when some of them end up committing a crime. Until we change how we treat kids on the front end, in the early days of their lives, too many others like those I met on that unforgettable day will continue to funnel through the system and never have the chance to dream of a better future. That is unacceptable.

It was also clear that the kids at the JJIC and Travis Hill School were self-aware: they knew they needed help; they also knew that without that help their lives might not materially improve. That same young woman at the detention center described how she sent home every dollar she earned working while in custody to support her struggling mother, who had six other children. How can we expect families to break out of this cycle of poverty without assistance? It shouldn't have to come from their kid who is locked up.

Similarly, other students at Travis Hill School recently submitted a video entry discussing the obstacles they face in their lives to the Aspen Challenge, which is a competition giving young people the tools to design solutions to social problems. And they won. In that video, they suggested that there should be biweekly family counseling sessions that would allow families to understand and explore and treat each other's grief and trauma. "The parents will learn skills . . . and will get the understanding of what trauma is, what grief is, like stress, anxiety," one student suggested.[17] Maybe we should start listening.

I now regularly use my platform to highlight the issues facing young people in this parish and state, and will continue to do so until we end the mistreatment of our kids in the legal system and close the education, literacy, and racial wealth gaps that low-income kids and kids of color face.[18] One thing that I am especially proud of is our McCollum Scholars Program, which provides four-year, need-based, $80,000 college scholarships to eligible students from New Orleans. But for some, moving from New Orleans to a four-year university somewhere else can be jarring. To provide long-term support and ensure those students' success, as part of the program they each receive a year of counseling to prepare for college. We continue to support these promising students throughout their time away, giving them access to academic coaches, mental wellness resources, and internship placement opportunities.[19]

From Inspiration to Action

Why do I do this work? Beyond what I saw when I was young and what I've observed throughout my life, I am inspired by Bryan Stevenson, one of our foremost advocates for racial justice and founder of the Equal Justice Initiative. When he speaks, he stresses the importance of recognizing everyone's humanity and treating each person on this planet with dignity. It's such a simple message but turns out to be so hard for many of us to practice. Yet he has followed his own advice consistently in his own work for decades, where he relentlessly fights to ensure that the most marginalized in our society receive fair treatment. He leads by example, even in some of the most impossible situations.[20] If he can do that full-time, in a place that doesn't always want to hear what he has to say, those of us who are lucky enough to have a platform—as we do in the NBA—can be similarly dedicated to pushing for a more just world.

Stevenson's example is one of the many reasons I am proud to have been elected president of the National Basketball Players Association (NBPA), the labor union of 450 athletes who are part of the NBA brotherhood. Every day, I am able to speak out on behalf of our membership, protect their rights in the workplace, and support their personal and professional growth. I'm also proud that the NBPA, the coaches' association, and the NBA league office came together to create the National Basketball Social Justice Coalition—a joint venture that institutionalizes our commitment to pushing for justice through policy and advocacy across the country. The Coalition members are all different and each care about different issues. We are not a monolith. Some want to push for improved voting rights or fight back against retrenchment. Others want to lobby for better education. Still others want to work toward a more equitable, less brutal, criminal justice system. But at the root of this Coalition, what binds and joins us together, is a shared desire to fight for everyone to be treated with dignity, no matter their race, education, religion, sexual orientation, or economic situation.

We've put forth an audacious goal. But so, too, was the goal of becoming an NBA player. If we can make it in the greatest league on earth, why should we stop there?

· 7 ·

STRONG COMMUNITIES
IN ACTION

JAMAHL MOSLEY

Head Coach, Orlando Magic
Board, National Basketball Social Justice Coalition

The Dream

What does it mean to live the "American dream"? I believe it's different for everyone, but from where my life was during the darkest times, it was definitely a far-reaching idea to think I'd ever become a head coach in the NBA.

After my mother became sick and eventually passed away in 2004 due to complications from multiple myeloma, I knew it was time to shift my dreams of playing professional basketball and focus on becoming a coach. Thanks to the kindness of some amazing coaches, I was able to be a volunteer intern with the Denver Nuggets. With each step up the ladder (intern, video department, scout, player development, assistant coach), my path to becoming the head coach for the Orlando Magic was one of many challenges and hard work, with a lot of help from others along the way.

I'm in a position now where achieving my goals and living my "American dream" can hopefully help provide guidance to others as they work to do the same in their own lives.

A Strong Community

It takes a strong community to win. And on our team, every player is fully aware of his own value as well as his teammates'. Those strong communities are even more important off the court. Regardless of what the loudest and most extreme voices in politics would have us believe, I have learned that we have more in common with our neighbors than we think.

I'll break it down to the community level. In Orlando, we root for the same teams. We use the same streets to get to work every day, enter the same grocery stores and coffee shops, drop our kids off at the same schools and parks . . . sometimes even complain about the same tourist habits, much as we love them! We all navigate the same physical, social, and cultural landscape. Most of us are worried about the economy, affordable housing, health care, and how we will provide for our families. We want to spend more time with our loved ones. We want a good life, our own version of the American dream, and we are all doing our best to make it a reality. We all contribute and deserve to have a say in the direction of our municipality, our city, our state, and our country. The same holds true about you and your neighbors—whether you look the same, speak the same way, or make the same amount of money.

That is especially true when it comes to the vote. We are all the same. And we have to protect the idea that everybody's vote matters equally. The idea of "one person, one vote" may not have originated in the United States, but it has become a bedrock of American democracy. It reminds us that, through our collective voting power, we can shape our country's destiny together. Every time we make it harder for people to vote, we fail to uphold and achieve the ideals of our democracy: the idea that no matter your political affiliation, no matter what issues you care about, no matter who you want to vote for, your right and ability to cast a ballot are sacred. Without that freedom, the dreams we are all chasing can start to slip away.

When we prevent certain members of our community from fully participating in democracy, it holds the entire community back. Being a father of three young children of my own, I want them all to feel that they are able to participate in our democracy and have confidence that their voices will be heard.

The NBA's Platform

The NBA has a uniquely powerful platform, and it is crucial that we continue to shine a light on the importance of civic participation. Our league has a younger, more diverse fan base than other professional sports leagues: 56 percent of our fans are under forty-four years old and 40 percent are people of color.[1] Across all sports, of the top ten most-followed U.S. athletes on social media, seven are NBA players: LeBron James, Stephen Curry, Kevin Durant, Russell Westbrook, Kyrie Irving, Chris Paul, and James Harden.[2] And the NBA has more than two billion social media followers watching our game.[3]

All of that translates to a singular opportunity to educate people on what is happening in their communities and inspire them to impact change.

In 2020, twenty-three NBA teams opened their facilities to help increase voting participation by using them as polling and voting registration locations.[4] The league doubled down on its commitment to civic engagement in 2022 with the decision to not play games on Election Day, not only to allow players, coaches, team employees, and staff to vote, but also to use that moment to promote the message of civic participation nationwide.[5]

Promoting civic participation and increasing access to voting are core goals for our team as well. Starting in 2020, we urged voters to register to vote and get to the polls with our campaign "Get Off the Bench. Get into the Game. Vote."[6] The campaign included a dedicated web page; a Vote.org partnership; public service announcements; voter toolkits; player and coach involvement; a social media education campaign; opening Amway Center as an early voting/voter registration location; and holding events to encourage voter participation.[7] In 2022, we continued our efforts; on National Voter Registration Day, we partnered with the Orange County Supervisor of Elections to host voter registration events at community gyms.[8] Players and former players participated, reinforcing the message that voting is the "first step" in shaping and changing our politics.[9] Magic leadership also encouraged staff to volunteer as poll greeters on Election Day.[10]

The Social Justice Coalition, the NBA community's policy and advocacy arm, helps lead our mission to drive change, and I'm proud to be a member of the Coalition board. It is our duty to actively encourage people to vote and, where we are able, provide them with the resources to do so. It is equally important that we raise the alarm when we see attempts to take away that fundamental right. We believe that every American should have more opportunities to contribute to our democracy. That should be the dream.

FIGHTING HUNGER, ONE DAY AT A TIME

LARRY NANCE JR.

Power Forward, Atlanta Hawks
Founder, Zero Hunger Challenge
Founder, Athletes vs Crohn's & Colitis (AVC)
Board, National Basketball Social Justice Coalition

Food Love

The minute I set foot in New Orleans, I knew it was a special place. Seventeen million people visit this city every year, so chances are you know someone who adores the city; who has felt the warmth radiating from the people they pass on the street; who has embraced its distinct culture, art, and music scene; who has maybe had a little too much fun at Mardi Gras, Essence Fest, Jazz Fest, or one of the many other special celebrations the city hosts.

And everyone—*everyone*—loves the food.

If you are lucky enough, someone in New Orleans will invite you over for some gumbo, likely a family recipe that has been passed down for generations. What I have learned, particularly being in

New Orleans, is that food often has a complex history. For example, the gumbo you eat, as well as the method by which the dish is prepared using a roux, is a result of the fusion of African, Native American, French, Spanish, and Caribbean people—all forced together by the transatlantic slave trade. As writer Nikesha Williams put it, "Gumbo, in a sense, is the best part of the worst moments of our history."[1]

Today, New Orleans's relationship with food is still complex. A city so well known for its cuisine struggles with food insecurity, meaning that there are too many New Orleanians who do not have enough to eat and do not know where their next meal will come from. In a country of such abundance, nobody should ever go hungry.

My Battle

I have probably spent more time thinking about food than the average person. At the age of sixteen, I was diagnosed with Crohn's disease, an inflammatory bowel disease. For several years before that, I lived with painful symptoms like cramping, weight loss, stunted growth, and chronic fatigue. I couldn't stay awake at home or in class, and I couldn't play sports. There is no cure for Crohn's, and in some people, it can lead to life-threatening complications.

I have had to think carefully about how to get protein because I can't rely on eating nuts and seeds throughout the day. I can't eat popcorn, raw vegetables, or spicy foods. I learned that I need to play on an empty stomach, and I'm now used to eating a shockingly heavy portion of steak and pasta at the end of every day to prevent weight loss. Had I not mastered the precise balance that works for my body, I would likely be nine inches shorter, one hundred pounds lighter, and most definitely not a professional athlete competing at the highest levels. Food is an integral part of my success.

My interest in food issues was also sharpened by my college curriculum. Before getting drafted into the NBA, I earned my degree in criminal justice from the University of Wyoming. I wanted to be a police officer growing up, and, as I got older, I planned to work in a forensics lab. But I had the chance to pursue a basketball career, something of a Nance family tradition. But my career as an athlete hasn't stopped me from thinking about the justice issues impacting the communities where I've lived and played. Quite the opposite. The deeper into my career I get, the more I feel a responsibility to help tackle the inequities that are around us each and every day. As a professional basketball player in a league with a fan base of 2.2 billion people worldwide, my platform is too big not to take advantage of.

A Justice Issue

The key point here is that food insecurity is a justice issue. Food is the most basic human need, and when people are food-insecure, they face severe consequences to their physical health, mental health, and well-being. In addition to malnutrition, people experiencing food insecurity are also more likely to experience chronic conditions like heart disease, diabetes, and high blood pressure.[2] Food insecurity can harm people's mental health, resulting in stress, anxiety, and depression.[3] It is well documented that when people do not have their basic needs met, they can experience social isolation, stigma, and shame.[4] Without enough food, people may struggle to maintain enough energy to perform basic life functions. Most concerning, if a child experiences food insecurity, the effects can be lifelong—impairing growth and development and resulting in unfavorable health behaviors in adulthood.[5]

Far too many people are going hungry in our country. According to national data, food insecurity is present in all counties, parishes, and boroughs.[6] More than 44 million people, including 13 million children, experience food insecurity in the United States. Latino and Black households are more than two times as likely to be food-insecure[7]—a sad irony given the deep influence of Black and Latino cuisines and food traditions on the American diet. During the COVID-19 pandemic, food insecurity spiked as businesses shut down, unemployment rates skyrocketed, and food supply chains were disrupted nationwide.

Food insecurity affects one in seven people in Louisiana. That means almost 700,000 people in Louisiana are regularly going hungry. This is more people than the populations of Shreveport, Baton Rouge, and New Orleans—the three largest cities in Louisiana—combined.[8] The depth of need is stunning.

In New Orleans, the second most food-insecure city in the U.S., 61,000 adults and 20,000 children live in households without enough to eat.[9] Almost 14 percent of seniors living in New Orleans are food-insecure.[10]

Natural disasters increase the risk and rates of food insecurity—and New Orleans is especially susceptible because of its geography. I arrived in the city a little over five months after Hurricane Ida made landfall in Louisiana as a Category 4 storm on August 29, 2021, exactly sixteen years after Hurricane Katrina. Although Ida's effects were not as severe, the city's power grid was damaged and more than a million people lost power for two weeks; as a result, most residents and food retail businesses lost their entire food supply. For residents who did not have the means or resources to leave, they risked food insecurity and short- and long-term impacts on their health.[11]

It is important to remember that rates of food insecurity are likely severely underreported, so we may not know the full extent of the problem.[12] Many federal and local government agencies only send out surveys on food insecurity once a year (or less frequently) to determine if people have experienced insecurity in the last twelve months; in cities where researchers conduct these surveys monthly, reported rates of food insecurity rise dramatically. Equally troubling, when conducting food insecurity surveys, the federal government only measures "how much we eat, not whether what we eat is good for us, our communities, and our environment."[13] Without a complete picture, any efforts to address food insecurity are at best incomplete.

Generational Change

My family legacy is proof that one generation can change everything. My father, Larry Nance Sr., played thirteen seasons in the NBA. He was a three-time NBA All-Star, was an NBA All-Defensive First Team member, and won the very first NBA Slam Dunk Contest in 1984; along the way, he scored 15,687 career points and grabbed 7,067 career rebounds. Despite those accomplishments, my dad will be the first to tell you that he never thought he would become a professional basketball player. I think about the world my father was born into and how it changed in just the first ten years of his life.

My father was born in 1959, five years after the civil rights movement to end legalized racial segregation, discrimination, and disenfranchisement in the U.S. began. He was just days away from turning one when four college students stood up against segregation in North Carolina and refused to leave a Woolworth's lunch counter without being served. He was four years old when Martin Luther King Jr. delivered his "I Have a Dream" speech to two hundred thousand people during the March on Washington on August 28, 1963. He was six in 1965 when six hundred peaceful protestors marched from Selma to Montgomery to express outrage about the killing of a Black civil rights activist by a white police officer and to demand legislation enforcing the Fifteenth Amendment, which in 1870 had granted Black men the right to vote. Those protestors were horrifically beaten and teargassed on a day now known as Bloody Sunday. That same year, President Lyndon B. Johnson signed the Voting Rights Act of 1965, banning all voter literacy tests and authorizing federal review of states' voting procedures to ensure that they were not discriminatory.

At eighteen, my father attended Clemson University, which had desegregated only fifteen years earlier.[14] While there, he was drafted into the NBA in the first round, even though he had always assumed he would be a truck driver and mechanic. Decades later, his sons—my brother Pete and I—born into a very different world, followed him into the league.

The story of the civil rights movement is one of great sacrifice—and great progress. American patriots put their bodies and lives on the line to fight for basic human rights. And we shouldn't forget that many of the movement leaders and participants responsible for key moments in history were very young. Those same students who organized the Woolworth's lunch counter sit-in ultimately helped launch the Student Nonviolent Coordinating Committee (SNCC) to encourage students to join the movement.

Another incredible example is the four thousand children who were involved in the Children's Crusade in Birmingham, Alabama; they revived the movement at a time when adults were increasingly unwilling to volunteer, get arrested, and risk losing their jobs.[15] These children walked out of their classrooms on "D-Day," May 2, 1963, singing "Freedom," setting off a week of mass demonstrations that resulted in the arrest of two thousand kids. As one historian said, the activism of children is "what broke the back of segregation."[16]

Zero Hunger Challenge

Since the 1960s, movements for racial justice, equality, community safety, and peace have been fueled, in large part, by this nation's young people. Knowing this and being aware of my platform and privilege as an athlete in the public eye, I have been driven to invest in the power, talent, and innovation of the next generation; in particular, I want to find the solutions that will make food insecurity a problem of the past. It is our responsibility to educate our young people about the potential and promise of their communities—and how to combat the systemic challenges that might stand in their way.

In November 2023, I launched the Zero Hunger Challenge campaign. I reached out to principals of New Orleans public high schools and presented an idea to engage their juniors and seniors to develop detailed plans to combat food insecurity in the city. The competition, which awards $10,000 college scholarships to each student from the winning team (a total of $50,000), provides civic-minded juniors and seniors with the opportunity to propose transformative solutions to food insecurity.

Students from six schools across the city met on February 4, 2024, to present their initiatives to a panel of judges that included me, Natalie Jayroe (CEO, Second Harvest of South Louisiana), Mannone Butler (Head of Programs & Partnerships, National Basketball Social Justice Coalition), Mike Katz (Benson Capital Partners), Dr. Avis Williams (Superintendent, NOLA Public Schools), Swin Cash (Pelicans VP Basketball Operations & Team Development), Dr. Darvelle Hutchins (Pelicans VP Equity & Social Impact), and Tifferney White (CEO, Louisiana Children's Museum).

On March 3, teams from four finalist schools—Eleanor McMain Secondary School, Sophie B. Wright Charter School, The Willow High School, and Frederick A. Douglass High School—presented their ideas. In true New Orleans fashion, participants and guests were treated to incredible food, made by local New Orleanian and James Beard Award–winning chef Nina Compton. Students presented plans that included revitalizing corner stores in neighborhoods, food distribution, and growing nourishing foods in one's own home. In the end, Frederick A. Douglass's "Keep It Growing" project, proposing educating people on growing their own food, was the winner. I was so impressed with the proposals that I awarded an additional $25,000 for the second-place team, Willow School.

The Zero Hunger Challenge reinforced for me that, when given the opportunity and the right supports, young people can and will rise to the moment. I look forward to helping these talented and innovative students implement their vision for a New Orleans where everyone has access to healthy food.

Root Causes

Justice requires all hands on deck.

We can't just rely on young people to put an end to food insecurity issues. Solving big problems requires collective action from government, corporations, foundations, community organizations, health care providers, and advocates. I have been grateful for the service of food banks, such as Second Harvest Food Bank of South Louisiana, that address the ongoing lack of access to food in the New Orleans region. Every year, Second Harvest distributes more than 32 million meals to over 200,000 people. However, food banks, soup kitchens, and other food distribution sites are only short-term interventions that meet the needs of people experiencing hunger now.

In case you missed this statistic earlier, I'll repeat: people struggle with food insecurity in *every county, parish, and borough* in this country.[17] So, food insecurity is everyone's problem to fix.

We must go beyond just helping people get food when hungry to addressing the root causes of food insecurity: poverty and unemployment, a lack of affordable housing, racism and discrimination, and lack of access to quality education and health care. Wherever you sit in this equation, I urge you to think about ending the injustice of food insecurity. To listen to what communities say about their hunger, what they need, and invest in their solutions. To create and offer quality jobs with livable wages and good benefits. To educate community members on nutrition, which will help them make more informed decisions about what they eat, not just when they eat. To lower the cost of higher education, a cost that often makes it difficult to get a quality job. To get serious about more data collection so we can all get smarter about the types of programs and policies we need to end hunger. To encourage and incentivize the brilliance, creativity, activism, and advocacy of our youth. And yes, to continue to donate to and volunteer at food banks and soup kitchens that play such a crucial role in community well-being while we work on these larger systemic solutions.

Second Chances

Justice requires us to think about those we have forgotten.

As a board member of the National Basketball Social Justice Coalition, I would be remiss to not mention the role of the criminal justice system in high rates of food insecurity across the nation.

Food insecurity is a frequently overlooked collateral consequence of incarceration. Although it is closely tied to more commonly discussed problems like houselessness and unemployment,[18] food insecurity has significant implications for returning citizens and their families. State by state there are thousands of barriers to employment and education for formerly incarcerated individuals, and they often struggle to find stable jobs and income. Without meaningful income, they cannot access healthy food. In fact, one survey conducted in three states revealed that 91 percent of formerly incarcerated individuals were food-insecure.[19]

Children of parents who are currently incarcerated are at especially high risk of experiencing food insecurity; one study showed that young children who live with their father before his incarceration are three times as likely to end up food-insecure. Another study found that "the incarceration of either parent increases the likelihood of food insecurity for adults and households with children by up to 15 percentage points."[20] The data make clear that incarceration and the barriers returning citizens face after they have paid their debt to society impact entire families and communities by denying their access to basic needs.

Employers and governments can be part of the solution. The Social Justice Coalition advocates for second-chance hiring, through which employers promote the benefits of employment and advance comprehensive strategies that actively recruit and hire returning citizens. We also believe that state governments across the country should examine policies related to reentry: states that still limit access to food programs for low-income families like the Supplemental Nutrition Assistance Program (SNAP) or food stamps because of former convictions should abandon this discriminatory practice and ensure that formerly incarcerated people—disproportionately members of food-insecure families—have access to transportation, housing, and employment opportunities. Now is the time to shrink and transform the harm of the criminal justice system in this country, not double down on policies that punish our communities.

Making Gumbo

Much of my justice work has been the result of asking questions about the world around me. I urge you to begin asking your own. How can we leave a drastically better world for the next generation? How can we use our privilege and platform to raise awareness? Or, to borrow from Nikesha Williams and end as we began, how can we take an issue that reflects the worst of our present and make a gumbo that shows us a brighter future? The answers are up to us.

KEEPING OUR PROMISES

_____

VIVEK RANADIVÉ

Chairman, Sacramento Kings
Board, National Basketball Social Justice Coalition

Bigger than Basketball

When I bought the Sacramento Kings in 2013, I laid out a mission statement for the team, which was to build a winning franchise that enhances the lives of those it touches and makes the world a better place. I've always believed in using basketball as a platform for good, and the tragic events of March 18, 2018, gave new urgency to this organizational pursuit. On this date, an unarmed young Black man, Stephon Clark, was killed by police in his grandmother's backyard. Our city erupted in an outpouring of grief and fury, with protests throughout the city to draw attention to issues of police violence and systemic racism. For several weeks, the community rallied to express their pain and anger, with the public outcries culminating outside of Golden 1 Center during Kings basketball games. In this moment, we were reminded of what mattered: a man lost his life, and a community was grappling with how to heal not just from that one shooting, but from a long history of traumas experienced by vulnerable communities. I knew we needed to listen—and to act.

My Promise

I took a microphone to the court and made a promise. "We recognize that it is not just business as usual. And we are going to work really hard to bring everybody together to make the world a better place, starting with our own community. We are going to work really hard to prevent this kind of a tragedy from happening again."[1]

I knew my words wouldn't be enough to heal the pain, but I wanted to be clear that in Sacramento things were different, and we were going to work alongside the community to be part of the solution. I meant what I said, although I imagine at the time many viewed it with skepticism. Words are empty promises until we act upon them. But from that moment on, I promised to use our platform to convene conversations and make real strides toward equity and racial justice. I knew the Kings were uniquely positioned to show Sacramento—and the world—how sports can be a catalyst for creating meaningful change.

Why I Care

I have always believed that it is a tremendous privilege and honor to own a professional sports team, and with that opportunity comes responsibility. This steadfast belief is rooted in my own personal journey—when I was a young boy my father was put in jail for warning that a new aircraft flown by Indian Airlines and made by the Indian government was unsafe. The memory of him in a jail cell for speaking his mind is etched into my soul and has rooted my steadfast commitment to advocating for free speech and the right of peaceful protests. This is one of the key reasons I am a huge advocate for civic engagement and launched Rally the Vote in 2018. This campaign was a first-of-its-kind nonpartisan coalition urging fans to register to vote. As we all know, voting for leaders at every level of government is a foundational step to ensure that our justice systems reflect the values of the communities they serve. The coalition has grown to more than fifty members across professional sports teams and leagues and reached over 50 million fans ahead of Election Day in 2020. I firmly believe that there is no greater privilege than exercising your right to vote—your vote is your voice in shaping the future. My life's work has been to use technology to enhance people's lives by eliminating friction, and what could be more fundamental than to "democratize" democracy?

Our Actions

In the weeks and months following the protests, my team and I led a series of conversations with community leadership, including civil rights leaders, elected officials, faith leaders, and youth. We hosted a youth forum with Kings players to help facilitate an open dialogue, and ultimately healing. As a result, we created the Kings and Queens Rise Co-Ed Youth Sports and Mentoring League in May 2018, in partnership with the Center at Sierra Health Foundation's Black Child Legacy Campaign and My Brother's Keeper Sacramento programs, to provide young people opportunities to engage in intercommunity activities during the summer months. The program recognizes that we cannot incarcerate our way out of violence and that to keep our communities safe, we must invest better in our youth. Through this program, we work with hundreds of young people annually, helping to prevent and interrupt the cycle of violence.

Meanwhile, the community of Milwaukee experienced deep unrest following the tasing and arrest of Bucks player Sterling Brown in relation to a parking violation. As a result, the Kings partnered with the Milwaukee Bucks in 2019 to produce Team Up For Change, an award-winning initiative that brings together athletes, community leaders, policy experts, and the business community to discuss how we can join forces in enhancing justice and equity in communities disproportionately impacted by racism. We also discuss how to invest better in those communities that need it. We've grown that program considerably to include multiple NBA and WNBA teams and have expanded our programming to directly reach youth and vulnerable communities.

Through our community-centric, mission-driven approach, the Kings are committed to showing how to lead with purpose, which is why it was so important that the NBA created the Social Justice Coalition in 2020. For me, a lot of the impetus came from the conversations I had with the legendary Joe Dumars and NBA players. Joe said, "You guys and the NBA have been generous with your wallets, but we need more than that. You know the president, the governor, the people making and implementing the laws—you have access to power. Help us get that so we can facilitate institutional change to bring equity." As the advocacy arm of the NBA community, the Coalition is working to advance social justice policy on criminal justice, policing reform, voting rights, and community safety. Collectively we understand that the NBA has tremendous power, and we are working together to raise awareness and take up issues that impact our communities.

Our Legacy

The Sacramento Kings are dedicated to convening conversations, giving back to our community, and sparking meaningful change. Throughout our history, sports have had the ability to bring people together, and can be a bridge across different communities that helps build trust and empathy so we can face hard truths and real challenges together. That means fighting against the injustices that impact those who live here. That's what it means to be a leader and an ally, and I am committed to continuing the fight for social justice.

LEARNING FROM HISTORY

GLENN "DOC" RIVERS

Head Coach, Milwaukee Bucks
Former Board, National Basketball
Social Justice Coalition

Today

Today, I live a life full of joy and good fortune. I've played the game I love in the best league in the world. I've coached legendary players and won a championship. I have healthy, beautiful children and grandchildren. I've lived in some of America's greatest cities. Every day, I feel lucky.

But, again and again, I've seen the darker side of the country I love, up close and personal. We are almost 180 years after the Civil War and nearly sixty years past the end of Jim Crow—and yet racism still plays a role in far too many aspects of American life if you are a person of color. Wealthy or poor, educated or not, if you are Black or brown in America, you will likely be treated differently at some point in your life. And for some, this differential treatment occurs every day. You might be denied your choice of house. Or you might be denied the same loans that others are able to get. Or, for example, you might be pulled over, arrested, and harassed more frequently. These aren't simply my perceptions; they are, sad to say, well-established facts backed by the experiences of millions, not to mention decades of research.[1]

And so, even as I recognize every day how fortunate I am, I also know how fragile life is for many people of color in this country. I know how far we still have to go to eradicate the harms of a society that sees Black people as less-than. It's why working toward social and racial justice is just as important as my day job as a coach.

Yesterday

I grew up in Chicago in the 1960s and '70s, the son of a police officer. Back there and then, racism was just another daily fact of life as Chicago was one of the most segregated cities in America. As a result, Dr. King identified it as the first northern city in his fight against the nation's massive inequality and he started the Chicago Freedom Movement there.[2] The American Nazi Party marched in Skokie, just north of Chicago, in 1976.

Although I heard an occasional slur while my all-Black high school basketball team played, the effects of racism became more apparent while I played basketball as a student at Marquette University in Milwaukee, a city with a 23 percent Black population.[3] Like Chicago, Milwaukee had problems. The city was heavily segregated. In 1976, twenty years after *Brown v. Board of Education*, a judge finally ordered the schools to integrate.[4] Describing the disturbing reasoning given by those who oversaw the system, the judge wrote: "I was astonished at the trial to learn from the testimony of the Milwaukee school officials that they honestly believed that twenty years after *Brown v. Board of Education of Topeka* . . . they could knowingly and intentionally operate a segregated school system because they believed it was educationally superior to an integrated system." The false idea of "separate but equal" that had been struck down under law was still alive and well as I arrived in the city.

In my freshman year at Marquette I met the woman who would one day become my wife, Kris Campion. It is an understatement to say that many in the community didn't embrace interracial relationships at that time. Someone slashed her tires and put a racial epithet outside of her parents' home in suburban Milwaukee. I can't express the trauma we experienced. For those fortunate enough to have never experienced it, racism isn't something people just brush off. You may carry on as normal outwardly; but those kinds of experiences stay with you a lifetime.

Personal and Professional

My time as a player in the NBA was a dream. I played eight years in Atlanta, two years in Los Angeles, three in New York, and ended my playing career with San Antonio. But, while the league is a special place, its history includes the same kinds of blind spots on inclusion that can be all too common in business. In the 1990s, the league averaged just five Black head coaches each season, despite a clear pipeline of people qualified for those positions. The front offices were also largely white and male. If representation matters at every level, especially at the top, many of us were getting the message that certain positions were not open to us. Today, the league has improved its record, recently scoring an "A" in the 2023 NBA Racial and Gender Report Card released by The Institute for Diversity and Ethics in Sport (TIDES).[5] The number of Black coaches peaked at sixteen in 2022, and there are currently thirteen Black head coaches; but there is still a lot of work to do at every level.

Two years after I retired from playing in the league, I experienced a very personal attack yet again. At the time, I lived with my family in a small community about twenty minutes outside of San Antonio. It was a beautiful neighborhood but not a particularly diverse community. One day while our family was out of town, our house was burned down. The entire thing, gone. One of our dogs was inside and didn't make it. I lost my photo albums (this was long before you could save everything digitally), my memories from my playing days, and of course, our home itself.

Was this crime racially motivated? I guess I will never know for sure, but the Texas Rangers believed it was.

Then there is the infamous Donald Sterling incident. For those who don't remember, Sterling owned the Los Angeles Clippers franchise from 1981 to 2014, and I coached there from 2013 to 2020. Even before the fiasco, those paying attention knew that Sterling had deeply troubling business practices and a history of discrimination documented in a variety of lawsuits and settlements with the U.S. Department of Justice. What was perhaps an inevitable reckoning happened during our 2014 playoff run, my first year as the Clippers head coach, when the website TMZ published voice recordings of Sterling making derogatory and racist comments about Black people—including the players who were part of the Clippers organization.[6]

Our players were distraught. The person who paid their salaries did not think they were good enough to associate with because of the color of their skin. I too was affected. The fans were deeply affected, with many calling our offices repeatedly, demanding that Clippers employees take a stand. Perhaps the only person who did not recognize the depth of harm he caused was Sterling himself. He tried to come to the game that night. We told him no. We had no authority to tell him no, but we did.[7] He stayed away, and we played, but our players wore their shooting shirts inside out in protest during the pregame warm-up, knowing that further action would be necessary.[8]

Then the commissioner, Adam Silver, showed his leadership and did the right thing, issuing Sterling a lifetime ban, which ultimately led to a sale of the team. Sterling was out.[9]

Breaking with the Past

That horrific experience revealed something important to me about the extent of racism in America. Our league is made up of the most incredible athletes on the planet, over 70 percent of whom are Black. And in the twenty-first century, the same thing I experienced as a college athlete nearly forty-four years ago remains true: as much as people may recognize Black professionals' talent on the court, off the court some of us are still denied the full dignity we deserve as human beings—who have feelings, values, and autonomy just like everyone else.

And that is why the global reckoning on racial justice in 2020 was as important as it was devastating. After Derek Chauvin murdered George Floyd, millions of people took to the streets in protest. They were brave. Police used tear gas and rubber

THE POWER OF BASKETBALL

bullets on protestors in Philadelphia, which the police chief later characterized as a grave error.[10] In Austin, Texas, police fired so-called "less-lethal weapons"—beanbags that expand and can cause serious injuries—at peaceful protestors, including a pregnant woman. Protestors' injuries included a fractured skull, a broken jaw, and a severe chest wound.[11] In Florida, legislators passed a law that would give people immunity if they drove over protestors with a car, all but approving the use of violence against those who take to the streets to protest injustice.[12]

Those individuals who came out night after night to protest didn't have access to the financial resources that we do at the NBA. They didn't have the huge followings that public figures do on social media. They didn't have agents and lawyers on retainer. Yet they knew the importance of demanding change and were committed to the cause. Like so many Americans, it was evident we had to make our voices heard. In the months following George Floyd's murder, much of the NBA community was, literally, in a very safe Bubble[13] in Orlando—where we would exert our collective power.

I'm proud of the work that arose as soon as we entered the Bubble. In the very first game, players knelt around the "Black Lives Matter" decals on the court during the national anthem to protest police violence. Players used their media conferences to talk about the tragic death of Breonna Taylor, shot in her room by police while she slept. My son Austin, who has played in the league, spoke passionately about the murder of Trayvon Martin, gunned down in a Florida neighborhood at just seventeen.[14] I used my own platform to encourage people to vote, trying to remind everybody that no matter what they care about, participating in the democratic process is our right and also necessary to make a difference in our nation.

But we weren't yet working as a unified force. Just a month and a half into our time in the Bubble, we witnessed another horrific police shooting. On August 23, 2020, in Kenosha, Wisconsin, a white police officer shot twenty-nine-year-old Jacob Blake, a Black man, seven times in the back as he stood in front of his three children. The shooting left him paralyzed. Once again, the video went viral. Once again, the country erupted in protests over the unnecessary and excessive use of police violence.[15]

We've seen too many of those recordings. In fact, in the year following the protests, officer-involved killings of Black people continued to increase. Black people account for 13 percent of the United States' population, but in 2021 they made up 27 percent of those fatally shot by police. That calculation does not include the number of Black men, women, and children shot by police who survive, only to suffer a lifetime of injury and trauma; nor does it account for all the other systemic injustices Black people experience at the hands of police in this country. We are stopped, searched, frisked, charged, and prosecuted at rates far higher than others.

I couldn't take it in that moment—and we shouldn't take it ever. Enough was enough.

Change in the Air

By then, nearly everyone in the Bubble understood that it was time to demand immediate change in policing—and in the way that this country treats people of color. We also need to eradicate the double standard in our legal system where prosecutors and the courts hold ordinary people accountable for the harm they cause but not the police. Some may perceive a tension between calls for police accountability and the ability of police to keep our communities and neighborhoods safe. The truth is, the two go hand in hand.

Police are best equipped to keep communities safe when they have the trust of those who live in the community they serve. When community members trust law enforcement, they are more willing to communicate and collaborate on crime and violence prevention efforts, resulting in safer streets for both the public and the police. But historically, police have too often relied on unnecessary force, particularly against Black and brown people, which has harmed the communities they serve and weakened trust. When the legal system holds officers accountable for these practices—which simply don't meet law enforcement's oath to protect and serve all communities—it sends a message about respect for the rights and dignity of all people. These solutions are easy to name, but, of course, harder to achieve.

There was tremendous pain in the nation and in the Bubble after we watched the Blake shooting, but we also doubled down on our commitment to fight together. Afterward, players did not just boycott their playoff games. Instead, players and coaches, including myself, gathered in a room to discuss what we could do. Then, with players on strike, we came up with a vision for action. Eventually, on November 20, the NBA, the NBPA, and the NBCA announced the first-ever National Basketball Social Justice Coalition, a 501(c)(4) joint venture between all three entities to advance systemic justice reforms across the country. I was proud to be a founding member of the Coalition's board.

The Future

I'm proud of the impact work we've done since our commitments in 2020—although it hasn't been easy, and change hasn't come as fast as any of us would have liked. It never does. The Coalition has supported nearly thirty pieces of legislation and seen eight of them pass—a pretty good win rate for the slow-moving machine of politics. The group has pushed at the federal level for police reform, for improved voting rights, and for humane policies that end, once and for all, the racist sentencing disparity between crack and powder cocaine. We know that these fights are long, and our community is committed. So, on top of the federal work, the Coalition has supported NBA players, coaches, governors, and executives across markets who are working at the state and local level to promote violence intervention and community safety in places where crime has risen; to demand better treatment of justice-involved kids in our legal system; to help those who were previously incarcerated and paid their debt to society to rejoin our economy; and to ensure all Americans, no matter their politics or their circumstances, are able to cast their ballot in free and fair elections. Our work is just beginning.

But, as we fight for change, we also must continue to remind ourselves of what came before. In America, we tend to have short-term memories about the harms that have occurred in this country—especially against marginalized groups. Sometimes, it's not forgetfulness—it can just be easier and more comfortable to skip over the most painful parts of our history. (For example, I did not learn about the 1921 Tulsa Race Massacre, where a white mob destroyed the most prosperous Black neighborhood in America, until I was an adult.) We have some serious catching up to do in our educational system.

To fill in this gap, I make sure that when I coach, I don't shy away from exposing players to all aspects of our country's history. When I coached the Philadelphia 76ers, we held our training camp in Charleston, South Carolina, once the centerpiece of the transatlantic slave trade. We went to the Old Slave Mart Museum, and to the Avery Institute of Afro-American History and Culture. I brought in historians to talk about the painful truth that happened there.[16] You don't have to be an NBA coach to take time with those in your circle to learn about our country's history. It's something we all can do.

In the NBA, we have busy day jobs, which are also night jobs and weekend jobs. But we are also very lucky to work in a league that millions of kids dream about joining one day. Lots of people in this country also have busy day, night, and weekend jobs. Some work two or three jobs at a time. And they still find the time to battle against the injustices that, sadly, are all too common even today. The stakes are too high to stay on the sidelines. I'm proud that the NBA community has taken a stance and put our resources behind the fight for racial justice. I will be in that fight for the rest of my life. And I look forward to seeing new generations joining us and pushing us further toward the justice we all seek.

· 11 ·

THE TIME IS NOW

TIERRA RUFFIN-PRATT

Guard, Washington Mystics, Los Angeles Sparks
(ret. 2022)
Founding Member,
WNBA Social Justice Council

Undrafted

On April 15, 2013, the WNBA held its seventeenth draft. It was a competitive year, with Brittney Griner, Elena Delle Donne, and Skylar Diggins-Smith at the top of the class. My record wasn't too shabby, though. At the University of North Carolina, I led the team in scoring, assists, and steals, and doubled my career scoring average during my last season. I scored 30 points— a career high—in the first round of the NCAA tournament. But on that day in April, thirty-six names were called, and mine wasn't one of them.

Immediately after the draft, Washington Mystics general manager—coach Mike Thibault called to invite me to the team's training camp, but he warned me that I needed to get in better shape to be able to compete. By the time I arrived at camp a month later, I was in the best shape of my life, twenty-five pounds lighter, and armed with intel on every player on the team. Every day at camp, I did everything necessary to stand out—playing great defense, rebounding, making sure no one could block or outplay me. On May 21, Mike pulled me aside before practice to share some news: I had earned my spot. My cousin Julian "Ju" Dawkins was the first person I texted.

Cousin, Best Friend, Teacher

Ju wasn't just my cousin. He was my best friend. More like brother and sister, we were born just a month and a day apart in 1991. He was the reason I started playing basketball. When I was six, he started playing for a recreational league team. And even though it was an all-boys team in an all-boys league, I tagged along. I was excited to play, and I played with him and all the boys until I was thirteen years old and realized that I had a real talent for the game. We were from Alexandria, Virginia, and Ju wanted to be like NBA great and Virginia native Allen Iverson when he grew up. But most of the time, Ju just hogged the ball and tried to make every shot. Taller than him until eighth grade, I was the natural rebounder. In the way that only brothers can do, Ju took credit for my accomplishments, saying, "She got that from me." But, throughout our lives together, whenever I won, he won. And he also hurt when I hurt. So, when my name wasn't called on April 15, Ju cried. Just a month later, I was able to tell him that our disappointment was a thing of the past: my dream was coming true, and he would be able to watch me play as a pro.

But by 5 a.m. the next morning, Ju was dead. He had been shot and did not make it. The best day of my life had quickly turned into a nightmare. Julian, just twenty-two years old, was killed by an off-duty sheriff's deputy.

It wasn't until we were teenagers that we started to witness police harassment and abuse. When we were younger, our community was majority-Black and close-knit; but once white people began moving into the neighborhood, issues that would have previously been resolved among neighbors at the community level were now complaints filed with the police as a first resort. This led to an increased police presence, and the officers would bother and threaten the Black kids in our neighborhood. To avoid getting into trouble with police, Ju and I found ways to stay out of the way. Basketball was a safe haven and kept us off the streets—the same streets that used to be a safe place for kids like us to play and just be.

Julian was loved by everyone—which is not something you can say about everyone from Alexandria. There were a lot of fierce rivalries between neighborhoods and between schools, but Ju had the type of magnetic energy that attracted folks. He could go anywhere and become friends with anyone. Because of who he had been, the whole city supported us as we grieved. To say I was heartbroken by Ju's death is an understatement—he was my brother, my best friend, my teacher, my mentor. I went back to work two days after his death because I knew it was what he would have wanted. During my years in the W, you could probably catch me talking to Ju while I played.

The System We All Live With

I wish I could say that my cousin's tragic death was my first experience with the criminal justice system. When I was six years old, my father was sentenced to prison for twenty-seven years. As part of his commitment to remedy the unfairness at the heart of the criminal justice system,[1] President Barack Obama commuted my dad's sentence in 2014—sixteen and a half years later and the year after I entered the league. Growing up without two parents was all I knew, but my mother did an amazing job raising me and my sisters.

Still, at the time, I didn't realize the outsize role the criminal justice system plays in family separation. Now I know that one in four Black children can expect to have their father incarcerated before they turn fourteen.[2] Most of these children will be sent to live with a family member, but many will end up in foster care.[3] Long-term, children with incarcerated parents are more likely to struggle with behavioral and mental health issues, homelessness, and academic performance, and tend to be at higher risk of interacting with the criminal justice system.[4] Although it's estimated that the U.S. spends more than $80 billion each year to house 2.3 million people in prisons, there are additional hidden costs shouldered by families like mine—particularly the women in those families—that include money spent on making visits and calls and sending care packages.[5]

Over the years, I learned that other WNBA and NBA players had their own experiences with the justice system. In 2019, Maya Moore, the league's 2014 Most Valuable Player, left the game to help overturn her friend (now-husband) Jonathan Irons's wrongful conviction. Irons was a poor Black teenager when he was convicted by an all-white jury in Missouri in 1998.[6] In 2018, Sterling Brown was on his way home from a friend's place when he stopped by a Walgreens drugstore for three minutes, parking across two spots reserved for people with disabilities. What should have resulted in a simple parking citation escalated into officers attempting to intimidate Brown. Officers tased him, punched him, kneeled on his neck, and stepped on him, making cruel jokes as they did so. At the time, Brown was just twenty-two years old. [7]

"Say Her Name"

Of course, the summer of 2020 will always be remembered as a turning point for racial justice in America. But WNBA players had already started raising awareness about police violence in 2016. After the murders of Philando Castile in Minnesota and Alton Sterling in Louisiana, the Minnesota Lynx wore shirts that featured the phrases "Change Starts With Us—Justice & Accountability" and "Black Lives Matter," the names of Castile and Sterling, and the Dallas police shield (to honor victims of the July 7, 2016 attack on the Dallas Police Department).[8] Despite the WNBA initially fining teams for these actions, I organized a Mystics protest where players wore Black Lives Matter shirts and refused to answer questions about basketball in conversations with reporters—and the WNBA rescinded the fines.

If I had to describe the morale in the WNBA in 2020 after more news of police killings, I would say it was low. Quite honestly, we were all fed up. Sick and tired of the complete disregard for Black life in this country, of being dehumanized and criminalized and paying for it with our lives. It seemed like Black people were always getting the short end of the stick and the statistics proved it: while we make up only 13 percent of the country, we face 21 percent of police contact, make up 33 percent of people incarcerated, and are over three times more likely to be killed by police than our white neighbors and friends.[9]

Also, Black women—like Breonna Taylor, who was shot in her apartment in Kentucky in March 2020 by police serving a "no-knock" warrant—were often excluded from the public conversation on police violence. It took several months for our deaths to register with the broader public, which reinforced for many of us how little we were valued in society. Regardless of our individual backgrounds, all WNBA players ended up with the same conclusion: policing needed to change, and with our platform and experiences, we should not stay silent.

In July 2020, the WNBA and Women's National Basketball Players Association (WNBPA) launched The Justice Movement platform and the WNBA/WNBPA Social Justice Council, which would function as a driving force behind necessary and continuing conversations about race, voting rights, LGBTQ+ advocacy, and gun control among other important justice issues. I, along with Layshia Clarendon, Sydney Colson, Breanna Stewart, A'ja Wilson, Satou Sabally, and others stepped up to lead the work. Our advisors included Alicia Garza (founder, Black Future Labs, activist, and cofounder of Black Lives Matter), Carolyn DeWitt (CEO, Rock the Vote), and Beverly Bond (founder/CEO, Black Girls Rock!). Through the leadership of the Social Justice Council, WNBA players called for action to address the policy issues highlighted by the African American Policy Forum (AAPF); convened activists, organizers, and elected officials; and promoted community education on the census and voting rights.[10]

The WNBA dedicated that 2020 season to seeking justice for the women and girls who have been the forgotten victims of police brutality and racial violence. During the season, we promoted "Say Her Name," an AAPF campaign[11] to honor the memories and tell the stories of Black women and girls who have been killed by police. The campaign continues to call for police accountability as well as investment in other forms of community safety and security (including mental health services, domestic violence services, shelters for people without homes, education, and more). We wore special uniforms with Breonna Taylor's name, as well as warm-up shirts that displayed "Say Her Name" and "Black Lives Matter." We had other on-court moments that raised awareness about other individual victims of police violence including Michelle Cusseaux, Kayla Moore, and Tanisha Anderson.[12]

The Wizards and Mystics also marched with community members on several occasions. In those moments especially, I felt confident that—compared to where we were in 2016—a broader multiracial cross section of our community had finally grasped the depth of injustice in our country and would remain committed to change, no matter how long it took.

By the Numbers

On average, police in the United States kill more than 1,000 people every year with lethal force, or guns.[13] Over the last decade, police killed an additional 1,000 people with so-called "non-lethal force," or tactics meant to stop people without killing them (for example, physical holds, Tasers, and body blows).[14] George Floyd's death remains one of the most prominent examples of nonlethal force being used to kill someone.[15] These numbers mean that, on average, police officers in America kill three people every day.

More people were killed by police in 2023 than any other year in the past decade.[16] More than a third (36 percent) of these killings involved people fleeing the police.[17] The year 2023 also brought more high-profile police fatalities, such as the beating of Tyre Nichols in Memphis at the hands of five police officers and the death of Niani Finlayson—who called 911 for help over domestic violence and was instead shot by officers—in Lancaster, California. The rise in officer-involved killings is deeply concerning, and as Samuel Sinyangwe, a data scientist and policy analyst who founded Mapping Police Violence, stated, "[it] demonstrates that the promises and actions made after George Floyd's murder don't appear to have reduced police violence on a nationwide level."[18]

As expected, racial disparities exist in both lethal and nonlethal deaths. Between 2015 and 2021, Black Americans were 2.5 times as likely to be shot and killed by police officers as white Americans.[19] In 2023, that number slightly rose to 2.6 times.[20] Native Americans were killed at a rate 2.2 times greater than white people, and Latinos were killed at a rate 1.3 times greater.[21] People of color were also more likely to be killed while running or driving away. From 2013 to 2023, 39 percent of Black people killed by police had been fleeing. The same is true for 35 percent of Latinos, 33 percent of Native Americans, 29 percent of white people, and 22 percent of Asian Americans killed by police.[22] What's more, most victims of police violence are young, between the ages of twenty and forty.[23]

In addition to the loss of lives, other incidents falling under the umbrella of "police misconduct" (for example, excessive force, illegal arrest, wrongful search) cost the public billions of dollars. In 2022, the *Washington Post* found that nearly 40,000 payments to settle claims of police misconduct at twenty-five of the nation's largest police and sheriff's departments totaled $3.2 billion.[24] Some of those settlements were massive— Minneapolis taxpayers paid the family of George Floyd a settlement of $27 million for Derek Chauvin's depravity; Louisville taxpayers paid $12 million to Breonna Taylor's family;[25] and Cleveland paid $6 million to the family of Tamir Rice, the twelve-year-old boy shot by police in 2014.[26]

The *Post*'s investigation also revealed that police officers were often repeat offenders and identified these officers by name for the first time. In total, more than 1,200 officers in the survey had been the cause of at least five payments, and more than 200 had ten or more. Officers whose conduct was at issue in more than one payment were the subject of almost half of the payments.[27]

Beyond money, which is never guaranteed, it is rare for families of victims to receive genuine justice. Few officers face accountability for these murders. From 2013 to 2022, 98 percent of police killings have not resulted in officers facing charges.[28] Our family is part of the slim 2 percent: after an arrest and trial, Craig Patterson, the sheriff's deputy who killed my cousin, received six years in prison for voluntary manslaughter.[29]

Reform, Transparency, Accountability

For justice to be realized, we desperately need systemic policing reform. We need to enforce higher standards for the people we pay to protect us, including requirements that police officers be trained on implicit bias and deescalation techniques. We need to pass laws that require law enforcement agencies to eliminate racial profiling. We need to stop the unnecessary use of force and end use of chokeholds and no-knock warrants.

We need more transparency about who is being stopped and arrested in communities. We need a national registry that compiles records on police misconduct, so we do not have to rely on journalism alone to know whether we are safe. We need to create citizen review boards to hold officers accountable for their misconduct. And we need to support families who, like mine, are hurting; we need to provide compensation that covers counseling, funeral or burial expenses, lost wages, and more.

In the years after George Floyd's murder, several cities and counties have begun to change how law enforcement protects public safety. For example, San Francisco now uses crisis response teams to respond to behavioral health calls instead of police, while Minneapolis and other cities committed to reduce police presence in schools.[30] States embraced change too; at least twenty-five statewide legislative reforms were enacted that would ensure "greater policy uniformity within each jurisdiction." These laws covered use of force, duty for officers to intervene and report police misconduct, and policies that would encourage the decertification of police officers who have engaged in misconduct.[31] Voters also called for change, passing eighteen ballot initiatives that will strengthen law enforcement oversight over time.[32]

Our Duty to Win

Speaking on a National Civil Rights Museum panel in 2024, relatives of George Floyd, Tyre Nichols, Trayvon Martin, and Eric Garner expressed immense frustration with policymakers who have either failed to pass police reform legislation or, worse, have actively invalidated laws that would reduce the number of police encounters that end in death.[33] In spite of this, those courageous people have pledged to keep on going to ensure that their loved ones did not die in vain.

In contrast, as headlines about racial justice dwindle, we've seen the previously widespread commitment to allyship falter and fade. Some of that is due to fatigue and frustration at the slow pace of change; some of it is a result of explicit backlash to calls for change.

As the data reveal, there is so much more to do. It's important to remember that justice in policing became a national conversation only ten years ago—so we haven't even begun to scratch the surface of what is possible.

Justice is not a one-season thing. It is not a trend. It is not a moment. To paraphrase Dr. King's words, the arc of the moral universe bends toward justice—but it does not do so without work. We cannot sit on the sidelines and expect change. There's more we can all do. There's more that *you* can do. I still believe that anything can happen if people continue to raise their voice and stand in solidarity with the Black community who are fighting for justice. We cannot win standing alone.

Ju was my aunt's only child. She has often said police violence stole her past, her present, and her future. Any hope for an extended family, of grandchildren, of great-grandchildren died with her son. True justice means that no other family has to suffer the same pain my family has.

Until there is true justice, we must fight for it. As so many of us affirmed at the marches we attended in 2020, "It is our duty to fight for our freedom. It is our duty to win."

THE BUSINESS OF DOING JUSTICE

CLARA WU TSAI

Governor, New York Liberty
Vice Chairman, BSE Global
Founder, Brooklyn Social Justice Fund

Off the Sidelines

Over the last several years, I have been repeatedly asked a version of the same question: Why do you spend so much of your time and resources on social impact initiatives?

One answer is that, after witnessing so many injustices in this country and being surrounded by people who fight day and night for better opportunities for all, I know I can't stay on the sidelines. But it's also very personal to me. Social justice and a commitment to democracy are essential themes of my upbringing. They are part of my DNA.

Road to Kansas

I am the proud daughter of Taiwanese parents who immigrated to America before I was born. They landed in one of the unlikeliest of places—Lawrence, Kansas. In many ways, my parents fit right into that college town. Lawrence revolves around the University of Kansas, where my father taught economics. I loved our town; Weaver's department store, the local fabric shop, Sarah's—places that are still there today.

Our family's life in Lawrence existed squarely within the university that is its lifeblood; to this day, it still has a total population under 100,000. And yet in many ways, we existed squarely outside of it—the most recent census data reflects that Lawrence is 77 percent white, 6 percent Asian, and 5 percent Black. In the 1960s, it was no different. Being Asian in the Midwest meant then—and still means today—that we stood out. Like many immigrant families, we assimilated into our community. But we also had our own customs in our household, traditions that we valued deeply and kept.

It wasn't until much later in life that I fully realized the complex web of ways that differences, real or perceived, can easily lead to disparate treatment—from the most subtle moments of interpersonal disconnect to the systemic injustices that we now know can have deadly consequences. After graduating from high school, I was fortunate to head west to attend Stanford University for my undergraduate and master's degree, and then move across to the other side of the country to go to Harvard Business School. That world-class education allowed me to launch the career of my dreams, which included working at American Express, the *New York Times*, and Taobao. I've seen the world, worked my way up the corporate ladder, and landed in a place that once seemed unfathomable: an owner of four professional sports teams.

But I also learned that an elite education and an enviable career does not mean an easy path. I am a woman working in industries dominated by men. For easy evidence of inequitable treatment you need only look at compensation data: the gender pay-gap for entry level positions, for example, is 18.4 percent in this country; and while that narrows as you grow in seniority, it is never eliminated.[1] Women are also valued less than men, who are given more growth opportunities and promoted with greater frequency. This isn't limited to just the corporate world—just look at the obstacles female athletes are still overcoming.

Brooklyn-Bound

Since we have been in Brooklyn, I've become attuned to how dramatically some differences, like race and gender, restrict upward economic mobility, social mobility, and life outcomes. One of the starkest examples is the Black–white wealth gap. The data overwhelmingly documents that, even when living in the same Brooklyn neighborhoods, Black Americans' wealth is just a fraction of the wealth of their white counterparts. Between 2019 and 2022, the nation's Black–white wealth gap increased by $49,950, with the median white family owning six times the wealth of the median Black family.[2]

Such a massive disparity is directly attributable to generations of discriminatory policies that divested from Black communities and kept them isolated and poor—policies like redlining, school segregation, and public assistance programs that disappear when people start to accumulate even just a little in savings or assets.

Without huge investment in communities that have been marginalized for so long, upward mobility is, to paraphrase Langston Hughes, nothing but a dream deferred.

Brooklyn's life expectancy gap is no less shocking: the borough's white residents will, on average, live ten years longer than their Black neighbors. Even access to healthy food is more limited in predominantly Black areas of Brooklyn, which are New York City's biggest food deserts.[3]

Zooming out to look at New York as a whole, Black young people are more likely to be poor, unemployed, or disconnected (defined as unemployed and not in school) at 1.2 to 1.5 times the rate of their peers, and Black male youth continued to have the highest mortality rate of any group.[4]

Across the city, white households have a median net worth of $276,900, whereas Black households have a net worth of $18,870. Surprisingly, when people receive an undergraduate degree, the gap actually gets worse: Black households with a bachelor's degree have an average net worth of $32,000. White households with a bachelor's degree have an average net worth of $443,619.[5]

I am committed to fighting for the economic mobility of all people across Brooklyn. As a daughter of educators, I firmly believe that access to quality education can be a centerpiece to achieving more in life, but the statistics show how far out of reach higher education is for so many. When you are living on $18,870 a year in this city, you are barely scraping by. Trying to make sure your kids are succeeding in school is hard enough for any parent; doing so when you are struggling to make ends meet is an order of magnitude tougher. Finding work, building personal economic security, and helping the next generation on a path to higher education, vocational school, or the workforce should not be the impossible task that it is for so many in our community. That is why we are investing in Brooklyn.

Investing in the Future

Following the protests in the wake of George Floyd's murder, my husband and I launched the Social Justice Fund, which focuses on infusing resources into our community. Specifically, I promised Brooklyn that I would work for racial justice while investing in the community's response to—and attempt to recover from—the COVID-19 pandemic. First, we promised to invest in the BIPOC communities in Brooklyn that have been harmed by systemic racism. In 2021, we launched the EXCELerate program, which gave extremely low-interest loans to BIPOC-led organizations trying to recover from the impact of COVID on their work and earning potential. We worked with Brooklyn.org to form the Just Brooklyn Prize, which honors local community leaders working in a myriad of ways to improve the lives of those around them. In 2022, we started BK-XL, a start-up accelerator program targeting underrepresented founders and entrepreneurs with the potential to launch successful new businesses in Brooklyn. We invested in twelve companies and provided them with business training over a ten-week period. We have supplemented arts programs in public schools across the city and—understanding that safe, well-designed public spaces where young people can congregate is essential to preventing violence and improving kids' quality of life—we renovated basketball courts in public parks across the borough.

I have also come to understand that economic mobility cannot occur unless we also address issues with our criminal justice system. A criminal conviction is an economic trap that goes far beyond the intended accountability: not only are people prevented from securing certain jobs in the future because of a conviction, but constant meetings with a parole officer after that person gets home from prison means they often cannot hold down a job that requires regular hours. Worse, an initiation into the justice system brings with it a host of fines and fees that formerly incarcerated people must pay as they are processed through the system, pushing mostly poor individuals further into debt. Unless we mitigate some of the worst harms of the criminal justice system, far too many people will never have access to the upward mobility and improved life outcomes that all of us deserve.

People of color are trapped in the criminal justice system at disproportionate rates. Police more often use stop-and-frisk tactics against Black people in New York.[6] In Brooklyn, Black people are convicted of felonies and misdemeanors at nearly seven times the rate of white people, and they are also arrested at higher rates.[7]

Reforming the System

To start to attack the problems in our justice system, in 2019, I helped form the REFORM Alliance. Our board of directors—where I'm joined by Jay-Z, Laura Arnold, Robert Kraft, Meek Mill, Michael Rubin, Robert Smith, and Mike Novogratz—were all motivated both by what we had experienced in our own lives, witnessed in our own communities, and, in particular, by the outrageous sentence imposed upon artist Meek Mill for popping a wheelie on a dirtbike, which a judge claimed violated the terms of his probation. Setting aside how ridiculous a sentence of incarceration is for a wheelie, Meek's situation highlighted the massive problems with our probation system. At the time he received that sentence in 2017, he was still on probation from a 2008 conviction.

Meek's story struck us all in different ways. For me it was a clarion call about the fundamental flaws in our system. If you are on probation for nine years, you can't move out of your state for a new job; you have to meet with a probation officer at a specific time—one that may conflict with what your employer needs from you. You still have an open criminal record and are virtually guaranteed to be excluded during most job application processes. And of course, the smallest of infractions can lead you right back to jail and prison. A few days in jail is enough to lead to a loss of a job and send that person back to square one in their attempt to work or go to school and live a productive life.

REFORM works to end some of the most pernicious practices in our justice system. We believe that by reforming parole and probation laws we can change the path to work and economic well-being for marginalized communities. We like to say that we are working to move people "from the justice system into stability."[8] And we are proud that our work has been instrumental in passing probation and parole reform bills in California, Pennsylvania, Mississippi, and Michigan.

Another area of focus for my work across BSE Global and the Social Justice Fund has been to support reentry initiatives. We've made significant grants to organizations leading on this work, and we have made important changes within our own workplaces. Before we assumed ownership of Barclays Center, the arena operator had a policy that prohibited hiring formerly incarcerated individuals until they were off parole or probation for seven years. We worked with our operator to change this policy so that we could help to increase employment opportunities for people coming out of the justice system.

THE POWER OF BASKETBALL

And finally, in 2023 BSE Global partnered with the REFORM Alliance to host a job fair at the arena. The fair served over two thousand New Yorkers, many of whom were justice impacted. Our work went beyond the event itself as well. In advance of the job fair, we held preparatory workshops for participating employers to teach them about the importance of "second chance" hiring practices and encourage them to adapt their policies so that people who were once incarcerated are not excluded from employment opportunities.

Playing Our Position

The NBA has a vast platform, and we can use it to push for change. That's why I'm proud to be an owner of the Brooklyn Nets and the New York Liberty at a time when the National Basketball Social Justice Coalition and the WNBA's Social Justice Council exist.

On the men's side, the Coalition is a joint venture of the NBA, National Basketball Players Association, and National Basketball Coaches Association, leading advocacy efforts across NBA markets with a focus on criminal justice, policing, voting rights, and community safety reforms. Supporting measures like New York State's Clean Slate Act, which Governor Kathy Hochul signed into law in November 2023, is just one example of the issues the Coalition drives on behalf of the NBA community.

On the women's side, the WNBA Social Justice Council addresses systemic racism, LGBTQ+ rights, voting rights, and other issues affecting women in the U.S. In its inaugural season, the Social Justice Council held community conversations and virtual roundtables, and hosted player-produced podcasts and other

activations on topics ranging from the history of inequality in the U.S. to implicit bias and systemic racism against Black and brown communities.[9]

As an owner of a WNBA team, I'm enormously proud of the work we've done to improve the working conditions of our female athletes at the New York Liberty. Over five years, we made investments in our players and their development. We moved our games from the Westchester County Center into the Barclays Center. We invested in performance staff, player wellness, and care. As a result, the Liberty became known as a team that deeply values and supports its players.

The Road Ahead

I'm a long way from Kansas. But what I learned there has informed every step I've taken my entire life. The lessons are pretty simple. Education is critical but too hard to access for too many people. Economic mobility is essential, but women and communities of color have been systemically held back. Sexism and racism are worse if you are already trapped in a cycle of oppression. We need to right the wrongs of discrimination and poverty in order to help people access the education and job opportunities they need to improve their lives. In the end, I believe that to whom much is given, much is required; so, for those of us privileged enough to be able to contribute and make change, it's imperative that we do so thoughtfully and consistently. Those lessons are not hard, and I believe that following them will help anybody leave their community a little better than they found it. I, for one, will honor them for the rest of my life.

ACKNOWLEDGMENTS

This collection would not be possible without the support of many people who not only support the impact work of the National Basketball Social Justice Coalition and the Vera Institute of Justice but consistently commit their time, talent, and energy to the difficult work of making the world a better place.

Special thanks to Ashley Combs, Bethany Donaphin, Drew Franklin, Taj McWilliams Franklin, Kiki Griffin, Cynara Lilly, Annemarie Loflin, Becky Beland McNaught, Paul Robinson, Nina Revoyr, Bonnie Thurston, and Erin Trowbridge for their tireless support of the authors and feedback on various drafts of the essays. Gratitude to Jessica Brand and the team at the Wren Collective for essential research and fact-checking support.

For their contributions throughout the development and production process, we thank our colleagues at the Vera institute of Justice, The New Press, Fox Hammer Digital, and Dix Digital Prepress and Design, including Nia Abrams, Maury Botton, Chris Choi, Fran Forte, Lindsey Nater, Kevin Mercado, Vivian Su, and Rachel Vega-DeCesario. Thanks to Eric Zohn at Grubman Shire Meiselas & Sacks, P.C. for the legal support. A very special thanks to Nick Turner for his constant support of this project from inception to execution. And deepest thanks to Marc Favreau, whose guidance, insight, proofing, and sheer know-how (along with his unflappable demeanor) kept our project moving along tough production deadlines.

We are indebted to all board members of the National Basketball Social Justice Coalition, past and present: Carmelo Anthony, Micky Arison, Steve Ballmer, Clay Bennett, J. B. Bickerstaff, Avery Bradley, Sterling Brown, Dwane Casey, Jrue Holiday, Andre Iguodala, Tre Jones, Jamahl Mosley, Donovan Mitchell, Marc Lasry, Larry Nance Jr., Lloyd Pierce, Vivek Ranadivé, Doc Rivers, Michele Roberts, Adam Silver, Ryan Smith, Mark Tatum, Karl-Anthony Towns, and Tamika Tremaglio.

We are also grateful to current and former colleagues across the NBA league office and NBPA executive office who supported this work from the beginning, including Mike Bass, Kathy Behrens, Chris Benyarko, Kelsey Boyd, Matt Carpenter-Dennis, David Dietz, Cathy Engelbert, Samantha Engelhardt, David Foster, Amanda Thorn George, Kurt Heinold, Chase Kressel, Brian Lee, Lyzz Ogunwo, Kori Davis Porter, Ira Reiss, Kelly Schrader, Erika Swilley, Lauren Ware, Jamila Wideman, Leah Wilcox, and Catriona Quinn.

The Power of Basketball could not have been developed without the input and ongoing work of the Coalition's team. A huge thanks to Abby Omojola for her efforts over many long days and nights in the production process. Our thanks to Brandon Gassaway for his timely and prescient policy and narrative insights, to Janice Tolbert for research support, and to Neha Patel for the endless logistical knots quickly untangled in service to this project. Finally, a very special thank-you to Mannone Butler, whose fingerprints can be found on virtually every element of this book across the development, drafting, and publication stages; her extraordinary contributions throughout ensured that this project progressed smoothly from inception to execution.

NOTES

Introduction by James Cadogan and Ed Chung

1. https://www.vera.org/news/research-shows-that-long -prison-sentences-dont-actually-improve-safety.
2. https://www.washingtonpost.com/investigations/interac tive/2022/police-misconduct-repeated-settlements/.

1. No Time To Waste

1. https://usafacts.org/.
2. https://opportunityinsights.org/paper/race/.
3. https://www.latimes.com/sports/clippers/story/2020-07 -08/steve-ballmer-group-foundation-clippers-owner-billionaire.
4. https://www.gunviolencearchive.org/.
5. https://wisqars.cdc.gov/fatal-reports, https://www.amer icanprogress.org/article/gun-violence-disproportionately-and -overwhelmingly-hurts-communities-of-color/.
6. https://www.bradyunited.org/resources/research/dispro portionate-impact-gun-violence-black-americans.
7. https://www.kff.org/other/poll-finding/americans-experi ences-with-gun-related-violence-injuries-and-deaths/.
8. Ibid.
9. Ibid.
10. Ibid.
11. https://vpc.org/studies/trauma17.pdf.

12. https://nicjr.org/wp-content/uploads/2021/06/DC-Land scapeAnalysisReport.pdf, pg. 3–4.

13. https://www.urbanpeaceinstitute.org/.

14. https://www.lagryd.org/.

15. https://detroitlive.org/.

16. DLIVE—Detroit Life Is Valuable Everyday (detroitlive.org).

17. https://safeandpeaceful.org/.

18. https://www.chicagocred.org/.

19. https://giffords.org/lawcenter/gun-violence-statistics /#:~:text=Gun%20homicide%20has%20a%20disproportionate,of %20the%20total%20US%20population.

20. https://www.politico.com/news/2022/12/06/guns-commu nity-violence-intervention-collaborative-00072630.

21. https://www.hyphenpartnerships.org/cvi-collaborative.

22. https://www.ojp.gov/program/cvipi.

23. https://www.cviecosystem.org/.

24. https://www.cviecosystem.org/what-is-cvi.

25. https://apnews.com/article/covid-health-business-united -states-violence-872139d05edb0f710514894e45f0288b.

26. Ibid.

27. https://thegrio.com/2024/04/16/3-things-we-learned -from-the-nationwide-drop-in-homicides/.

28. https://policingequity.org/gun-violence/34-cpe-case -study-gun-violence-reduction-oakland/file.

29. https://abcnews.go.com/US/gun-violence-america-newark /story?id=79148257.

30. https://www.americanprogress.org/article/frequently-ask ed-questions-about-community-based-violence-intervention -programs/, https://cvg.org/impact/.

31. Ibid, https://giffords.org/lawcenter/state-laws/investing-in -local-intervention-strategies-in-connecticut/.

32. https://www.juvenilejusticeresearch.com/sites/default/files /2020-08/GRYD Brief 2_The Impact of the GRYD IR Program_6.20 20.pdf.

33. https://news.northwestern.edu/stories/2023/11/chicago

-community-violence-intervention-program-shown-to-reduce
-gun-violence/.

34.   https://www.washingtonpost.com/opinions/2023/11/22
/community-programs-reduce-gun-violence/.

35.   https://urbanlabs.uchicago.edu/attachments/a62ee
6577262a53b83e54b14ba4a1995bccbe9be/store/8b89a14e
657c8ae9268ef3c72333c7043cca2bbc29c57478f24720b
00cb6/READI+01.2023.pdf.

36.   https://www.cjactionfund.org/.

2. Doing the Work

1.   https://www.sandiegouniontribune.com/sports/sports
-columnists/story/2021-02-11/bernie-bickerstaff-usd-san-diego
-basketball-nba-cleveland-cavs-cavaliers.

2.   https://www.bellarmine.edu/magazine/article/magazine
-2021/2021/10/28/nearly-60-years-after-the-war-on-poverty
-why-is-appalachia-still-struggling/.

3.   https://www.psychiatry.org/getattachment/6494c34d
-26ea-47f1-956e-c45a99464247/Position-Police-Brutality-and
-Black-Males.pdf.

4.   Ibid.

5.   https://www.ncbi.nlm.nih.gov/pmc/articles/PMC6292675
/#:~:text=Studies%20examining%20trauma%20exposure%20
among,.%2C%202010%3B%20Centers%20for%20Disease.

6.   https://www.ncbi.nlm.nih.gov/pmc/articles/PMC62
92675/.

7.   https://www.ncbi.nlm.nih.gov/books/NBK207191/#:~:text
=Delayed%20responses%20to%20trauma%20can,with%20the
%20trauma%2C%20even%20remotely.

8.   https://www.nba.com/cavaliers/release/time-to-talk
-200623.

9.   https://www.healthline.com/health/repressed-emotions
#physical-effects.

10.   https://www.brennancenter.org/our-work/research-reports
/voting-laws-roundup-2023-review.

11. https://www.nba.com/cavaliers/releases/rmfh-polling-location-200811.
12. https://theathletic.com/2083079/2020/09/22/its-not-partisan-its-everybody-cavs-host-voter-registration-event-at-arena/.
13. https://www.rocketmortgagefieldhouse.com/events/vote.
14. https://www.vera.org/beyond-jails-community-based-strategies-for-public-safety.
15. https://signalcleveland.org/cleveland-mental-health-co-response-team-says-new-approach-is-helping-people/.
16. https://www.news5cleveland.com/news/local-news/report-clevelands-poverty-rate-improving-but-city-still-worst-in-u-s-for-child-poverty.
17. https://www.communitysolutions.com/more-reliable-2021-census-estimates-have-erased-progress-on-cleveland-childrens-poverty/.
18. https://nbacoaches.com/coaches-for-racial-justice/#:~:text=The%20National%20Basketball%20Coaches%20Association,of%20and%20teaching%20the%20history.
19. Ibid.

3. The Question That Drives Me

1. https://web.archive.org/web/20121004213304/http://tps.cr.nps.gov/nhl/detail.cfm?ResourceId=1610&ResourceType=District.
2. https://batten.virginia.edu/about/news/alum-action-education-malcolm-brogdon.
3. https://savingplaces.org/we-are-saving-places?gad_source=1&gclid=CjwKCAjwmYCzBhA6EiwAxFwfgNIxS6-KvWFtGOozKUyJwiz2vfBUP-IohavkrUhbZ9BDQEwYSVFfLBoCYCoQAvD_BwE.
4. https://www.georgiatrust.org/.
5. https://www.instagram.com/berniceaking/p/C2I7QVsrmCN/.
6. https://blogs.baylor.edu/faithsports/2020/06/08/john

-hurst-adams-church-leader-and-civil-rights-icon-and-also
-malcolm-brogdons-grandfather/.

7. Ibid.

8. Ibid.

9. https://www.bu.edu/sth/files/2019/09/Rev-John-Hurst
-Adams-Funeral-Book.pdf.

10. https://blogs.baylor.edu/faithsports/2020/06/08/john
-hurst-adams-church-leader-and-civil-rights-icon-and-also
-malcolm-brogdons-grandfather/.

11. https://www.thestate.com/news/local/article194255979
.html.

12. https://archives.library.sc.edu/repositories/3/resources
/963#:~:text=Bishop%20John%20Hurst%20Adams%20(1927,
to%20assist%20the%20black%20community.

13. https://www.thestate.com/news/local/article194255979
.html.

14. The flag remained on state grounds until 2015, however.
https://eji.org/news/confederate-flag-removed-from-south-car
olina-state-house/#:~:text=The%20Confederate%20battle%20
flag%20outside,other%20African%20Americans%20during%20
Bible.

15. https://blogs.baylor.edu/faithsports/2020/06/08/john
-hurst-adams-church-leader-and-civil-rights-icon-and-also
-malcolm-brogdons-grandfather/.

16. https://www.slamonline.com/the-magazine/oscar-robert
son-essay/.

17. Ibid.

18. Ibid.

19. Ibid.

20. https://www.npr.org/2016/06/10/481523465/in-political
-activism-ali-pulled-no-punches-and-paid-a-heavy-price.

21. https://www.aclu.org/muhammad-ali.

22. Ibid.

23. https://www.npr.org/2022/08/01/1114795613/racial-jus
tice-pioneer-nba-bill-russell.

24.   https://www.npr.org/2022/08/01/1114795613/racial-justice
-pioneer-nba-bill-russell#:~:text=After%20Medgar%20Evers
%20was%20murdered,Cleveland%20to%20meet%20with%20Ali.

25.   https://arthurashe.com/pages/legacy#:~:text=But%20he
%20was%20also%20a,sportsmanship%3B%20and%20an%20
American%20hero.

26.   https://arthurashe.ucla.edu/2010/07/04/apartheid-exclu
sion-and-ashe-south-africas-complicated-history-in-interna
tional-sports/.

27.   https://www.cnn.com/2022/06/24/us/arthur-ashe-citizen
-ashe-hiv-aids-activism-cec/index.html.

28.   https://www.bostonglobe.com/2023/03/31/opinion/juvenile
-justice-should-focus-rehabilitation-not-punishment/#:~:
text=We%20can't%20ignore%20the,%2C%202023%2C%20
3%3A00%20a.m.

29.   https://time.com/6092807/chris-paul-nba-strike/.

30.   https://www.sportspromedia.com/insights/interviews/nba
-foundation-greg-taylor-charity-black-community-interview/.

4. Telling My Story For Good

1.   https://harvardlawreview.org/print/vol-136/stacked-where
-criminal-charge-stacking-happens-and-where-it-doesnt/.

2.   https://caronbutler.com/news/sb-nation-former-clipper
-caron-butlers-tuff-juice-story.

3.   https://www.youtube.com/playlist?list=PLV6T9XP6FyOJ8
_6H2qioEO8R1N_SMyxW6.

4.   https://www.wishtv.com/lifestylelive/former-nba-all-star
-caron-butler-co-authors-shot-clock-young-adult-book-se
ries/.

5.   https://www.sentencingproject.org/policy-brief/youth-just
ice-by-the-numbers/.

6.   https://nij.ojp.gov/topics/articles/examining-relationship
-between-childhood-trauma-and-involvement-justice-system.

7.   https://www.sentencingproject.org/reports/why-youth-in
carceration-fails-an-updated-review-of-the-evidence/.

8. https://www.sentencingproject.org/reports/effective-alternatives-to-youth-incarceration/#footnote-ref-115.

9. https://www.sentencingproject.org/reports/why-youth-incarceration-fails-an-updated-review-of-the-evidence/.

10. Ibid.

11. https://www.sentencingproject.org/reports/effective-alternatives-to-youth-incarceration/#footnote-ref-115.

12. https://www.urban.org/sites/default/files/publication/99228/evaluation_report_on_new_york_citys_aim_program.pdf.

13. https://johnjayrec.nyc/wp-content/uploads/2011/07/yapfacts201401.pdf.

14. https://www.sentencingproject.org/reports/effective-alternatives-to-youth-incarceration/#footnote-ref-47.

15. https://www.mstservices.com/our-community, https://www.fftllc.com/sites

16. https://www.sentencingproject.org/reports/effective-alternatives-to-youth-incarceration/#footnote-ref-115.

17. Ibid.

18. https://www.sentencingproject.org/reports/why-youth-incarceration-fails-an-updated-review-of-the-evidence/.

19. https://www.sentencingproject.org/publications/protect-and-redirect-americas-growing-movement-to-divert-youth-out-of-the-justice-system/#footnote-ref-5.

20. https://www.sentencingproject.org/reports/diversion-a-hidden-key-to-combating-racial-and-ethnic-disparities-in-juvenile-justice/.

21. https://www.sentencingproject.org/publications/protect-and-redirect-americas-growing-movement-to-divert-youth-out-of-the-justice-system/#footnote-ref-5.

22. https://solitarywatch.org/facts/faq/#:~:text=Solitary%20confinement%20cells%20generally%20measure,live%20lives%20of%20enforced%20idleness.

23. https://www.detroitnews.com/story/sports/nba/2021/06/07/ex-nba-player-caron-butler-works-end-solitary-confinement-prisons/7594433002/.

24. https://www.prisonlegalnews.org/news/2023/jan/1/new-connecticut-law-restricts-use-solitary-confinement/#:~:text=The%20new%20law%20limits%20all,for%20more%20than%20five%20days, https://ctmirror.org/2023/05/30/ct-strip-search-prison-end-bill-study/.

25. https://www.ncsl.org/civil-and-criminal-justice/states-that-limit-or-prohibit-juvenile-shackling-and-solitary-confinement.

26. https://www.sentencingproject.org/policy-brief/juvenile-life-without-parole-an-overview/.

27. https://imprintnews.org/justice/raise-age-where-legislation-stands-final-three-states/52186. Louisiana recently repealed its Raise the Age law during a 2024 Extraordinary Session, https://apnews.com/article/louisiana-jeff-landry-crime-bills-3f985b6d8abefda715da6e54d9ef608a.

28. https://info.mstservices.com/blog/juveniles-right-to-attorney#:~:text=No%20state%20guarantees%20juveniles%20access,free%E2%80%9D%20court%2Dappointed%20lawyer.

29. Ibid.

30. https://www.nytimes.com/interactive/2021/05/24/us/tulsa-race-massacre.html.

31. https://innocenceproject.org/tough-on-crime-policies-are-at-odds-with-the-presumption-of-innocence/.

5. For Our Children

1. https://www.texastribune.org/2023/12/05/uvalde-officer-student-trainings-mass-shootings/.

2. https://www.nytimes.com/2022/07/10/us/uvalde-injured-teacher-reyes.html.

3. https://www.texastribune.org/2023/12/05/uvalde-officer-student-trainings-mass-shootings/.

4. https://www.nytimes.com/2022/07/10/us/uvalde-injured-teacher-reyes.html.

5. Centers for Disease Control and Prevention, National Center for Health Statistics. WONDER Online Database, Underlying Cause of Death. A yearly average was developed using four years of the most

recent available data: 2018 to 2021. Everytown For Gun Safety Support Fund, "EveryStat: United States," https://everystat.org. Based on analysis of 2019 HCUP nonfatal injury data.

6. https://harris.uchicago.edu/files/uchicago_harris_ap_norc_poll_report_final.pdf.

7. https://everytownresearch.org/report/the-impact-of-gun-violence-on-children-and-teens/.

8. Ibid.

9. https://everystat.org/wp-content/uploads/2019/10/Gun-Violence-in-Texas-2.pdf.

10. https://www.ksat.com/news/local/2020/08/06/report-san-antonio-ranks-4th-among-us-cities-with-biggest-increase-in-homicide-rates-in-2020/.

11. https://publichealth.jhu.edu/center-for-gun-violence-solutions/solutions/community-violence-intervention#:~:text=Community%20violence%20intervention%20(CVI)%20programs,%2C%20disinvestments%2C%20and%20trauma%20occur.

12. https://www.vera.org/community-violence-intervention-programs-explained, https://www.vera.org/inline-downloads/community-violence-intervention-programs-explained-report.pdf.

13. Ibid., Ibid.

14. https://www.sa.gov/files/assets/main/v/1/samhd/documents=/violence-prevention-strategic-plan.pdf.

15. https://www.texastribune.org/2024/01/17/san-antonio-violence-public-health/.

16. https://www.washingtonpost.com/parenting/2023/03/29/america-gun-violence-parenting/.

17. Ibid.

18. https://apnews.com/article/nba-sports-basketball-texas-tre-jones-8660b12913e9422f486f3321fc7f621d.

19. Ibid.

20. https://everytownresearch.org/report/gun-violence-trauma/?_gl=1*t3it4m*_ga*OTY2MTY2MzAOLjE3MTAzMzU4NDE.*_ga_LTOFWV3EK3*MTcxMDM0OTkyNS4yLjAuMTcxMDM0OTkyNS4wLjAuMA.

21. https://everytownsupportfund.org/new-research-and-stra
tegies-on-gun-violence-trauma/.

22. https://www.axios.com/2023/04/17/majority-americans
-mass-shootings-stop.

23. https://everytownresearch.org/report/the-impact-of-gun
-violence-on-children-and-teens/.

24. https://everytownresearch.org/report/gun-violence-tra
uma/#opportunities-to-better-support-survivors-of-gun-vio
lence.

25. https://allianceforsafetyandjustice.org/wp-content/up
loads/2023/09/ASJ-NATCRIMEVICTIM23d.pdf.

26. https://everytownsupportfund.org/new-research-and-stra
tegies-on-gun-violence-trauma/.

6. Finding the Path

1. https://www.rstreet.org/commentary/bipartisan-consen
sus-on-juvenile-justice-crumbles-in-louisiana/.

2. https://www.nolacypb.org/wp-content/uploads/2020/02
/Called-to-Care_Jan2020.pdf.

3. https://www.ncbi.nlm.nih.gov/pmc/articles/PMC3968319
/#:~:text=This%20landmark%20study%20suggests%20that,trau
ma%20%5B13%2C%20136%5D.

4. https://www.nber.org/digest/jan07/does-child-abuse
-cause-crime.

5. https://www.bigeasymagazine.com/2020/01/22/report
-finds-child-trauma-rates-higher-than-soldiers-returning-from
-war-in-new-orleans/.

6. https://www.splcenter.org/20160217/more-harm-good
-how-children-are-unjustly-tried-adults-new-orleans.

7. https://www.fox8live.com/2023/12/13/new-la-task-force
-aims-tackle-juvenile-incarceration-rates/.

8. https://cfsy.org/sentencing-children-to-life-without-pa
role-national-numbers/#:~:text=At%20the%20peak%20of%20
JLWOP,sentences%20over%20the%20past%20decade.

9. https://static1.squarespace.com/static/55bd511ce4b083

0374d25948/t/5600cc20e4b0f36b5caabe8a/1442892832535
/JLWOP+2.pdf.

10. https://thelensnola.org/2023/05/10/louisiana-leads-nation
-in-percentage-of-people-in-adult-prisons-for-crimes-they
-committed-as-kids/.

11. https://www.thedailybeast.com/angola-aka-louisiana
-state-penitentiary-is-ordered-to-move-youth-out-of-adult
-prison.

12. https://www.aclu.org/press-releases/judge-orders-louis
iana-to-remove-children-from-angola-prison-by-september
-15.

13. https://www.rstreet.org/commentary/bipartisan-consen
sus-on-juvenile-justice-crumbles-in-louisiana/.

14. https://justicepolicy.org/wp-content/uploads/2022/02
/sticker_shock_final_v2.pdf.

15. https://lakidsrights.org/we-advocate/.

16. https://andscape.com/features/new-orleans-pelicans
-guard-cj-mccollum-asks-how-to-help-black-youths-in-the
-city/.

17. https://www.cbsnews.com/news/incarcerated-students
-win-award-for-mental-health-solution/.

18. https://www.si.com/nba/pelicans/news/cj-mccollum
-named-nba-cares-bob-lanier-community-assist-award
-winner.

19. https://bleacherreport.com/articles/10105188-pelicans-cj
-mccollum-announces-scholarship-program-for-new-orleans
-hs-students.

20. https://news.wfu.edu/2023/02/24/face-to-face-with
-bryan-stevenson-the-opposite-of-poverty-is-justice/.

7. Strong Communities in Action

1. https://www.sportsbusinessjournal.com/Articles/2024/03
/19/nba-playfly-sports-vision-insights-report.

2. Ibid.

3. Ibid.

4. https://www.nba.com/nba-arenas-polling-place-voting-center-2020-election.

5. https://www.nba.com/news/qa-cj-mccollum-james-cadogan-on-the-importance-of-election-day.

6. https://www.nba.com/magic/orlando-magic-continues-its-efforts-encourage-central-florida-get-bench-get-game-vote-20200915.

7. Ibid.

8. https://www.clickorlando.com/results-2022/2022/08/16/orlando-magic-promote-elections-voting-with-new-campaign/.

9. https://www.nba.com/magic/news/mo-bamba-continues-to-encourage-people-to-vote-and-make-their-voices-heard-20220920.

10. Ibid.

8. Fighting Hunger, One Day at a Time

1. https://www.eater.com/2020/1/13/21056973/where-did-gumbo-originate-dish-history-new-orleans.

2. https://www.feedingamerica.org/sites/default/files/2023-07/FA_HealthEQ_Closer-Look_AHG_final_updated-stats.10132021\.pdf.

3. Ibid.

4. Ibid.

5. Ibid.

6. https://acrobat.adobe.com/link/track?uri=urn%3Aaaid%3Ascds%3AUS%3Af0ac6e9a-f3c3-3f00-832e-dbd1304646a9.

7. https://www.ers.usda.gov/webdocs/publications/102076/err-298.pdf?v=7508.8.

8. https://www.feedinglouisiana.org/hunger-in-louisiana.

9. https://www.hhs.gov/.

10. https://www.feedingamerica.org/sites/default/files/2023-04/State%20of%20Senior%20Hunger%20in%202021.pdf.

11. https://www.ncbi.nlm.nih.gov/pmc/articles/PMC9489999/.

12.   https://www.sciencedirect.com/science/article/pii/S0749379723001629.

13.   https://blog.ucsusa.org/alice-reznickova/food-insecurity-is-a-bigger-problem-than-our-government-thinks/.

14.   https://documentinghistory.clemson.edu/studentprojects/s/clemson-integration-desegregation/item/1049.

15.   https://www.history.com/news/childrens-crusade-birmingham-civil-rights.

16.   Ibid.

17.   https://acrobat.adobe.com/link/track?uri=urn%3Aaaid%3Ascds%3AUS%3Af0ac6e9a-f3c3-3f00-832e-dbd1304646a9.

18.   https://www.prisonpolicy.org/blog/2021/02/10/food-insecurity/.

19.   file://Users/AOmojola/Downloads/rcc_final_report.04.29.22_0%20(1).pdf.

20.   https://uknowledge.uky.edu/cgi/viewcontent.cgi?article=1024&context=ukcpr_papers.

9. Keeping Our Promises

1.   https://sports.yahoo.com/kings-owner-offers-remarkable-speech-healing-compassion-154246647.html.

10. Learning From History

1.   https://www.ncbi.nlm.nih.gov/pmc/articles/PMC6864380/, https://www.smithsonianmag.com/history/158-resources-understanding-systemic-racism-america-180975029/.

2.   https://digitalcommons.law.udc.edu/cgi/viewcontent.cgi?article=1146&context=udclr.

3.   https://city.milwaukee.gov/ImageLibrary/Groups/cityDCD/planning/data/pdfs/UrbanAtlasPopulation.pdf.

4.   https://www.jsonline.com/story/life/2024/02/07/important-moments-in-wisconsin-and-milwaukee-black-history/72426206007/.

5. https://apnews.com/article/nba-lapchick-tides-report -card-ec54de6761b253d3c824a0e09fb60593.

6. https://www.espn.com/nba/story/_/id/27414482/when -donald-sterling-saga-rocked-nba-changed-forever.

7. https://www.cnn.com/2023/11/23/sport/poppy-harlow -doc-rivers-interview-spt-intl/index.html.

8. https://www.cbsnews.com/losangeles/news/clippers-turn -jerseys-inside-out-in-silent-protest-against-sterling/#:~:text =They%20huddled%20together%20at%20center,It's%20just%20 us%2C%20only%20us..

9. https://www.usatoday.com/story/news/usanow/2014 /04/29/donald-sterling-fine-penalty-racism-audio-commissioner -adam-silver-los-angeles-suspension/8460575/.

10. https://www.inquirer.com/news/philadelphia/philadelphia -lawsuit-settlement-police-response-2020-protests-2023 0320.html#:~:text=In%20an%20event%20that%20garnered, gas%20into%20the%20fleeing%20crowd.

11. https://www.kvue.com/article/news/local/police-protest -injuries-austin-police-bean-bag-rounds-ammunitiion/269-6f 2b64a9-40e7-49ad-a093-4be152746345.

12. https://www.vice.com/en/article/88n95a/florida-anti-riot ing-law-will-make-it-much-easier-to-run-over-protesters-with -cars.

13. https://www.usatoday.com/in-depth/sports/2020/07/09 /nba-bubble-takes-shape-disney-world/5387760002/#:~:text =The%20NBA%20has%20made%20a,current%20standings%20 in%20each%20conference.

14. https://www.espn.com/nba/story/_/id/29555143/nba-re start-how-nba-bubble-become-platform-social-justice.

15. https://www.nytimes.com/article/jacob-blake-shooting -kenosha.html.

16. https://www.postandcourier.com/sports/citadel/why -doc-rivers-brought-his-nba-76ers-squad-to-charleston-for -training-camp/article_5dc655e6-3ea9-11ed-b319-035ab 38e49f1.html.

11. The Time is Now

1.   https://obamawhitehouse.archives.gov/issues/clemency.

2.   https://www.nytimes.com/2018/06/22/us/family-separa tion-americans-prison-jail.html.

3.   Ibid..

4.   Ibid.

5.   https://www.themarshallproject.org/2019/12/17/the-hidden -cost-of-incarceration#:%7E:text=Prison%20costs%20taxpay ers%20%2480%20billion,some%20families%20everything%20 they%20have.&text=Every%20month%2C%20Telita%20Hayes%20 adds,State%20Penitentiary%20for%2028%20years.

6.   https://fivethirtyeight.com/features/maya-moore-gave-up -more-to-fight-for-social-justice-than-almost-any-athlete/.

7.   https://www.theplayerstribune.com/articles/sterling-brown -milwaukee-police-racial-injustice, https://amp.cnn.com/cnn/2020 /11/10/us/sterling-brown-milwaukee-settlement-spt.

8.   https://www.espn.com/espn/feature/story/_/id/29439678 /nba-wnba-players-decade-demanding-justice.

9.   https://www.brennancenter.org/our-work/research-reports /state-policing-reforms-george-floyds-murder.

10.   https://www.wnba.com/news/2020-season-long-commu nity-assist-award-all-wnba-players.

11.   https://www.aapf.org/our-demands.

12.   https://www.wnba.com/news/wnba-announces-a-2020 -season-dedicated-to-social-justice.

13.   These incidents include situations where a person is killed by law enforcement when they are labeled as having a mental health crisis, as well as "off-duty" incidents, although 97 percent of incidents occurred while a police officer was acting in a law enforcement capacity. Description of methodology: https://map pingpoliceviolence.org/methodology.

14.   https://apnews.com/article/associated-press-investigation -deaths-police-encounters-02881a2bd3fbeb1fc31af9208b b0e310, https://apnews.com/projects/investigation-police-use-of -force/all-cases/.

15. https://apnews.com/article/associated-press-investigation-deaths-police-encounters-02881a2bd3fbeb1fc31af9208bb0e310.

16. https://mappingpoliceviolence.org/?gad_source=1&gclid=CjwKCAjwmYCzBhA6EiwAxFwfgAIFJLgiKEgK_tT9mcrQm6aPxJrziRlUYBml_moH3DT5QrlYBxlTdxoCESYQAvD_BwE.

17. https://www.theguardian.com/us-news/2024/jan/08/2023-us-police-violence-increase-record-deadliest-year-decade.

18. Ibid.

19. The Sentencing Project, One in Five: Disparities in Crime and Policing, 2023, https://www.sentencingproject.org/reports/one-in-five-disparities-in-crime-and-policing/.

20. https://www.theguardian.com/us-news/2024/jan/08/2023-us-police-violence-increase-record-deadliest-year-decade.

21. Ibid.

22. Ibid.

23. https://www.washingtonpost.com/graphics/investigations/police-shootings-database/.

24. https://www.washingtonpost.com/investigations/interactive/2022/police-misconduct-repeated-settlements/.

25. Ibid.

26. https://fivethirtyeight.com/features/police-misconduct-costs-cities-millions-every-year-but-thats-where-the-accountability-ends/?itid=lk_inline_enhanced-template.

27. https://www.washingtonpost.com/investigations/interactive/2022/police-misconduct-repeated-settlements/.

28. https://www.theguardian.com/us-news/2024/jan/08/2023-us-police-violence-increase-record-deadliest-year-decade.

29. https://www.washingtonpost.com/local/crime/arlington-deputy-convicted-of-voluntary-manslaughter-in-may-shooting/2013/12/13/11d4e942-634b-11e3-a373-0f9f2d1c2b61_story.html.

30. https://www.cnn.com/2020/06/28/us/police-out-of-schools-movement/index.html.

31. https://www.brennancenter.org/our-work/research-reports/state-policing-reforms-george-floyds-murder.

32. Ibid., https://www.americanprogress.org/article/progressive-criminal-justice-ballot-initiatives-won-big-2020-election/.

33. https://apnews.com/article/police-violence-tyre-nichols-george-floyd-2c05e0950c21421e72d5135242b060d2.

12. The Business of Doing Justice

1. https://www.naceweb.org/job-market/compensation/nace-research-pay-inequity-based-on-gender-begins-at-the-start-of-career/.

2. https://www.federalreserve.gov/econres/notes/feds-notes/greater-wealth-greater-uncertainty-changes-in-racial-inequality-in-the-survey-of-consumer-finances-accessible-20231018.htm#fig1.

3. https://www.law.georgetown.edu/poverty-journal/wp-content/uploads/sites/25/2022/05/GT-GPLP220016-1.pdf-Silvia-Radulescu.pdf.

4. https://www.nyc.gov/assets/cidi/downloads/pdfs/2021-disparity-report-update.pdf.

5. https://comptroller.nyc.gov/wp-content/uploads/documents/The-Racial-Wealth-Gap-in-New-York.pdf.

6. https://www.nyclu.org/en/stop-and-frisk-data.

7. https://www.nyclu.org/en/news/racial-disparity-across-new-york-truly-jarring#:~:text=While%20in%20Brooklyn%2C%20the%20largest,and%20convicted%20of%20offenses%20at.

8. https://reformalliance.com/about/#.

9. https://www.wnba.com/news/wnba-announces-a-2020-season-dedicated-to-social-justice.

ABOUT THE EDITORS

James Cadogan is the Executive Director of the National Basketball Social Justice Coalition. He lives in Washington, DC.

Ed Chung is the vice president of initiatives at the Vera Institute of Justice. He lives in Washington, DC.

Publishing in the Public Interest

Thank you for reading this book published by The New Press. The New Press is a nonprofit, public interest publisher. New Press books and authors play a crucial role in sparking conversations about the key political and social issues of our day.

We hope you enjoyed this book and that you will stay in touch with The New Press. Here are a few ways to stay up to date with our books, events, and the issues we cover:

- Sign up at www.thenewpress.com/subscribe to receive updates on New Press authors and issues and to be notified about local events.
- Like us on Facebook: www.facebook.com/newpress books.
- Follow us on X: www.x.com/thenewpress.

Please consider buying New Press books for yourself; for friends and family; or to donate to schools, libraries, community centers, prison libraries, and other organizations involved with the issues our authors write about.

The New Press is a 501(c)(3) nonprofit organization. You can also support our work with a tax-deductible gift by visiting www .thenewpress.com/donate.